The Bubba Chronicles

For Jen,
Oh no not
Bubbas!

SELINA ROSEN

ISBN 1-893687-13-9

Yard Dog Press
710 W. Redbud Lane
Alma, AR 72921-7247

Cover art by James Hollaman

First Edition: August 2000

The following stories are
dedicated to the bubbas of the world --
misunderstood and underappreciated.
For without them, cars would stop running,
toilets would stop flushing,
and Jerry Springer would go off the air.

Contents

AND THAT'S JUST THE WAY IT WAS.

INTRODUCTION

I guess everybody's got a slightly different definition of what a bubba is. Some Concs (people from Key West) call themselves bubbas, but that's a regional thing. For most of us a bubba is a "good ole boy." He isn't too terribly politically correct. He likes to hunt and fish and ride four wheelers, and he has tools even though he doesn't always know how to use them.

The average bubba can't cook unless it's something that can be grilled, and doing the dishes is beyond him unless you can wad it up and put it in the trash – and even then he has to be reminded. Sex is great, but probably not as important as going on a camping trip or watching TV, especially if there's a big game on.

He not only hasn't seen a *GQ*, but has no idea what one is. Even if he did, he'd no doubt rate it as "a magazine fer sissies." His idea of getting really dressed up is shaving and putting on a shirt that has to be tucked in. He might do this if the wife reminds him that it's "her" anniversary, and he's planning on taking her out for a big night on the town – a movie and a trip to Burger King. If she's real sweet, he might even let her get everything double sized!

He loves his family, his mom and his pickup – not necessarily in that order. In many cases he has bound his waist (much in the way that Japanese women used to bind their feet), so that he wears the same thirty-two inch waist size that he wore at age fourteen. He allows his immense beer gut to grow over the top of his pants, thus creating what he proudly refers to as a "shed for his love machine."

Women can be bubbas, too, but they have to work harder to be accepted into the pack, and the minute they do any "sissy girl stuff" or say any of that "libber crap," they are voted right out. A female bubba must understand that she can hang with them only as long as she remembers that if no wives are present she has to go to the cooler and get them a beer.

You don't have to be southern to be a bubba, but it helps. Herein lies part of the problem with selling bubba stories. People who have never seen or lived with and around bubbas simply don't find them to be believable characters. Since most of your big time editors and publishing houses are up north (that's what we southerners call anything above the Mason-Dixon line), where there is a considerable lack of bubbas, few editors will accept these stories.

This is a shame because it means that there is a lack of good bubba fiction on the market today, and bubbas are very inventive and interesting characters. For instance, give a bubba a pocket knife and a bottle of bar-b-cue sauce, and he'd be the last one standing on "Survivor."

Why have I become such an expert in the field of bubbas? Simply, this is what any good mother does when her child has been stricken with a serious illness. You do research so that you can help your child live as full a life as possible. Yes, that's right – one day my son and his buddy drove up on their four wheelers in their camouflage coveralls after a day of deer hunting and asked me to get them a beer. I was quite shocked as realization crept over me. Somehow, try as I might to expose him to cultural diversity and Chinese food, my only son had become a bubba! At first there was the denial – *My son – a bubba?* Then there was the anger – *My son isn't a bubba!* Then the quiet acceptance – *My son is a bubba.*

I embraced his problem, and in helping him – mostly by cleaning fish and handing him tools while he worked on his pick up – I learned that bubbas are people, too. I then went to work and wrote these bubba stories. I turned our family's trouble into triumph, and if I can help just one person deal with their child's affliction, then my work is done. ◆

So, I wrote this for an anthology titled <u>Prom Night</u>, but they didn't take the story because they had already taken one similar to it. The other story was written by Gary Jonas, one of my best friends. I think that when you read this piece you'll agree that it's pretty scary that we think so much alike. It was inspired by the actions of my son and his friends, and a real incident with a windstorm.

Even a bubba needs a date for the prom, and he'll take just about anybody... or anything.

Prom Date
by Selina Rosen

Derek knew it was going to be a bad day when he saw the lawn was covered with the flowers from the cemetery again. Their farm was right across the street from one of the biggest grave yards in the area, and every time there was a bad wind they woke up to find ugly sun bleached plastic flowers and wreaths all over the yard.

His granddad always said that a strong wind blew in spirits. Of course after he said it he always blew a big fart and laughed, but Derek knew there was some truth to what the old shit said anyway.

He kicked a gaudy purple and yellow plastic flower encrusted cross out of the way and stepped off the porch. He looked up at the sky; it was dark gray, splashed with pink. Derek frowned. It was damn near the same color as that sick cow's tongue. The cow smelled awful bad, and just the thought of that stench made him want to chuck the sweet blue crunchy stuff he'd eaten for breakfast. He wished the damn thing would just die so that he wouldn't have to help his grandfather drench her even one more time.

He made his way down to the street to wait for the bus. Everybody else had wheels. Derek had wheels, too, for a while until he'd farted around driving too fast and not really watching where he was going. The next thing he knew his pickup truck was lying on its top in Clear Creek, and he was swimming in water so cold that his balls never had dropped back down where they belonged. Now he had to ride the bus with all the stupid grade school, middle school, and junior high kids. The only other high school kids that rode the bus were a couple of retards.

He had the worst luck in the world. That was all there was to it.

He heard the motorcycle before he saw it. He waved big, and his friend Meyer pulled in and stopped.

Meyer popped his helmet off and turned off his motorcycle. "Hey, Stowe. How's it going? See you've been decorating your yard with graveyard flowers again."

Stowe was Derek's last name; he got it from his daddy. That was all he'd ever gotten from him. His mother had dumped him on his grandparents when he was less than a year old, and two years later she'd dropped off his sister, Betty. No one had seen or heard from her since.

"How do you think it's going?" Derek shook his head in disbelief.

"I didn't know it was a quiz, man." Meyer laughed.

Meyer was probably the only Jew in Arkansas. At least he was the only Jew Derek knew. He certainly didn't live up to any of the TV stereotypes. His family was damn near as broke as Derek's, and Meyer made even worse grades than Derek did. But he was huge, good looking, and had a reputation with the girls for being "very sweet." Derek's sister Betty said Meyer was "the bomb," whatever the hell that meant. And God knew the shithead never had any trouble getting a date.

"I bought tickets, man! Cost me everything I made last month. I bought that suit..."

"At a yard sale!" Meyer interjected.

"I still had to buy it, and what for... So I can go to the prom alone. If only Jenny had waited just a couple of more weeks..."

"To die!" Meyer screeched in disbelief. "Man, I can't believe you! Your girlfriend blew her brains out, and all you care about is that you bought an extra prom ticket."

"She wasn't really my girl friend. Hell, I hardly knew her."

"You knew her well enough to ask her to the prom," Meyer said in numb disbelief.

"Ah, come on, Meyer! I was desperate. You know that. I needed a girl to take to the prom. And not just any girl – she had to be a *pretty* girl, so I could show all those ass hole preps that I'm not a loser. When she said yes... she was so pretty I thought... Wow! Look at me! I'm someone! Then she killed herself, and I look like an even bigger loser than I did before."

"Oh, poor Derek," Meyer said sarcastically. "Don't you even want to know why she did it?"

"Oh, I know why she did it. To make my life a living hell."

"You are really fucking warped," Meyer laughed without amusement. "Jenny's killed herself just to inconvenience you. Now that's some fucking ego you got there, Stowe."

"Hey, she's *dead!* Things can't get any worse for her. But look at me. I can't get a date for the prom because every girl thinks I'm a heel for even asking, because my *girl friend* just died. And all the guys are teasing me that I'm such an ugly bastard a girl would kill themselves rather than go out with me. To make matters worse, her mother keeps calling me up wanting to know if she told me anything. Hell, she didn't tell me nothing. What do they think we had, some deep conversation or shit where I asked *So, ever think of killing yourself?* and then she said *Yes, I think about it all the time.* It wasn't like that. Like I said, I hardly knew her. I thought she was cute; I would have fucked her after the prom if I got half a chance, but it wasn't like we were *serious* or nothing."

Derek followed Meyer's eyes. He was looking over at the graveyard at the still barren pile of dirt where Jenny was buried.

"I talked to her," Meyer said in a far away tone. "She was nice. I wish I knew... Wish there was something I could have done."

He sounded really sad, too. Derek supposed that was why all the girls thought he was so sweet. It had something to do with him actually *thinking* about shit like that.

"Me, too, because then maybe I wouldn't be going to the prom alone," Derek said with a laugh.

"You're an ass hole," Meyer said. Without getting off the motor bike he punched Derek in the shoulder with enough force to knock him back a few feet.

Derek caught himself just short of falling. He rubbed at his shoulder. "Hey, dick head, that hurt!"

"Good," Meyer said putting on his helmet.

He reached to start his bike, and Derek grabbed his arm just as he was about to turn the key. "Hey! Take me to school so I don't have to ride with all the freaking kids and retards."

"You know I can't," Meyer said. "My mom would have a cow. Besides, she took the extra foot pegs off my bike so I couldn't ride anyone else."

"Come on, man... I'll hang on real tight, hold my feet out..."

"I don't even have an extra helmet," Meyer said.

"So what, your old bag won't know."

"Don't call my mom names, ya pencil dicked bastard," he poked Derek hard in the chest with his finger. "And the old bitch WOULD know. She always knows every time I do something she tells me not to. I'm going to the prom tonight with Tasha, and I'm not going to screw it up by getting grounded. Ta, ta." He started the bike and roared off.

Derek watched him go.

His sister Betty ran out of the house, but slowed down to a crawl when she realized the bus wasn't there. She walked up next to Derek and started putting on her make up.

It was always the same thing with her. Sleep till the last possible minute, jump up, get dressed, and then running down the street after the bus or in the bus she put on her makeup. Today the bus was running a little late, so she was doing it in the yard.

He didn't know why she bothered. He was by no means a handsome boy, but she was by all definitions the ugliest girl he had ever seen. His grandmother kept saying she'd grow into her features and be gorgeous some day, but then grandma thought the tulip cut tires that went around her fruit trees and the cement menagerie on the front yard were pretty, so what the hell did she know?

Betty had lots of boy friends because she put out. If she didn't put out, no one would have given her a second glance. As it was, she was one of the most popular girls in the school. She was ugly, had bad acne, couldn't sing, couldn't dance, was overweight and had BO, but none of that mattered because she would do anyone, anytime, anyway. Grandma and Grandpa didn't have a clue. They thought she was a perfect angel, and that he, Derek, was the problem child.

That was what really sucked. He would like to be the demon spawn of Satan that his grandparents thought he was, but his little chicken shit job down at the Dairy Dump didn't make him enough money to buy any troubles. And without wheels... The only trouble he ever got in was for talking too much in his classes or getting in a scuffle.

Derek would happily put out till his dick fell off, but being willing to put out didn't win you any popularity contests when you were a guy. Life was so unfair.

He looked over at the graveyard longingly. Jenny had been so pretty. She had a pretty smile too, and he thought maybe that she had even really liked him. He would have been so proud to walk in there tonight with Jenny on his arm.

He'd thought about not going to the prom at all, but when they'd told him that the tickets were not refundable, the thought of having paid out all that money for nothing had made him want to hurl more than the sick cow's breath, so he had to go. Besides, the only thing more pathetic than going to the prom stag was not going to the prom at all.

The bus pulled up then, smoking and puttering. The engine sounded like it might blow at any minute. The door opened, and they got on. Derek could smell the exhaust fumes *in* the bus. He went to the back where the fumes were the worst and sat in his assigned seat, like all the other *kids*. As soon as the bus started to move the fumes dissipated, and he was almost sorry. Just a few more seconds of that shit and he would have asphyxiated, then he wouldn't have to go to the prom alone or hear one more crack about how a girl would rather kill herself than go out with him.

He looked out the back window and took one more look at the dirt on Jenny's grave. He looked away and out the side window. He saw the sick cow lying on her side in the pasture, deader than a doornail – whatever the hell that meant. He was thankful for that. At least he wouldn't have to deal with her smelly ass anymore.

The retarded girl he had to sit next to started talking to him the way she always did, and he wished he were as dead as Jenny and that cow.

"Hi, Derek. Are you going to the prom? I'm going to the prom. Would you like to go with me?" She smiled at him her crooked retard smile.

The kids all over the bus started laughing; the little bastards had put her up to this. He gave them all a dirty look, and they shut up. He forced a smile and looked at her. "I'm sorry, Summer, but I just wouldn't feel right, not with Jenny just dying and all. But thank you."

Derek was a little shocked at himself. He had been nice! It would have been easier to have been mean, but he was nice. He guessed maybe his grandma *had* taught him a couple of things, and not being mean to retards was one of them.

Life wasn't fair! What was a nice guy like him doing going to the prom alone? He looked at the retarded girl again. Maybe he had been too hasty in turning Summer down after all. Maybe any girl was better than no girl at all. If it was real dark, and he squinted his eyes, and she was all cleaned up and wearing a nice dress...

She turned and grinned at him then. There was something green caught between her rotten teeth, and drool was running down her chin. "That's OK, Derek, I understand."

Derek sighed and looked past her out the window. "I am the most pathetic human on the face of the planet."

The bus barely made it to school, and they were late, with all of the wonderful trimmings that went along with being late when you're in high school – even if it isn't your fault.

When he finally got to his first period class, Wild Dave popped him in the head with his pencil. "Where the hell were you, man?"

"The fucking bus was screwed up," Derek said rubbing the back of his head. He hated being littler than all his friends. They were always punching each other or thumping each other. The difference being that it didn't seem to *hurt* any of them.

"Maybe you should have had your granny drive you to school,"

Dave teased.

"Maybe you'd like to bite my ass!" Derek spat back a little too loud. The teacher sent he and Dave to the principal.

"You stupid fuck," Derek whispered at Dave.

Dave just grinned back. "Loosen up, Stowe. We've already passed. This is all just a formality. So we sit here instead of in class, big fucking deal."

"So, if we get in any real trouble they won't let us go to the prom," Derek said.

Dave shrugged. "There not going to kick us out of the prom because we talked in class. Whitters is a grade 'A' dick head, but even he's not stupid enough to do that."

"What do you mean?" Derek asked.

"Are you crazy, man? My mama would come down here and stomp his ass if he stopped me from going. She's already rented me a tux and got her video camera all warmed up."

"Who you going with?"

"Lindsey." Dave looked around then and lowered his voice. "I wanted to ask Cathy Redding, but I was too chicken shit. Lindsey and I decided to go together so that we wouldn't have to go stag, but we're not together, if you know what I mean."

Derek thought he did. Lindsey was sort of one of the gang. He wished he had thought to ask her first. It seemed like everyone had a date for the prom but him and Summer.

"Am I going to look too pathetic going alone?" Derek asked.

"Nah, nobody expects you to have a date this soon after your girlfriend died," Dave said.

"She wasn't my girlfriend!" Derek screamed.

"OK... All right! Geez!" Dave said.

They got called into the principal's office then.

Derek had no idea how long Whitters talked or what he said. The short ugly Neanderthal looking bastard just droned on and on and on.

"... remember, you're seniors now. Only four weeks away from graduation; after that you're on your own, boys. The Real World. Do you think any boss is going to let you lollygag around all day doing nothing, and making idle chatter? No! He's going to expect you to work. You've had a free ride, but now that ride is over. Do you understand what I'm saying?"

Dave raised his hand and Derek cringed.

"What is it, Mr. Watson?" principal Whitters asked, obviously out of patience with kids and life in general.

"Just what is lollygagging? It sounds bad, sir, and I'm pretty sure I've never done it..."

"Just get out of here!" he screamed.

They left the office.

The day got worse after that. For once he was only too glad to get on that bus. Whatever had been wrong with it had been fixed. As they started down the road, the rain finally started to fall. It started pouring down in buckets so that the bus had to drive about two miles an hour. A sports car whizzed by them going fast. There were three guys in the car and his sister Betty. She was an unbelievable slut, but at least everyone liked her. At least she wouldn't have any trouble getting a date for her prom when the time came.

At home he learned what he already knew... that the sick cow was now a dead cow. He tried to act sad, and was able to at least fool his grandparents.

It was only 4:30. Still hours till the prom. Way more than enough time to talk himself out of going.

Grandma had announced that Betty was eating at Monica's house, and so the three of them sat down to dinner.

"We had a spirit wind last night," his grandfather said conversationally.

"Herman! Don't you dare break wind at this dinner table!" his grandmother screamed.

Derek laughed, and almost spit mashed potatoes out of his mouth. His granddad laughed, too. Then got all serious.

"I was serious, Ma. That's what got ole Bossy. The spirit wind. It blows life out of the living and into the dead."

"Oh, fiddle-dee-dee," his grandmother said. "Don't start up with that foolishness again. You'll give the child nightmares."

"He's not a child anymore, Ma, he's a man. Damn near finished with high school. Hell, he's driving."

"Till I totaled my truck. That reminds me, Grandpa. You said I could take the truck tonight, but I don't think I'm going. I mean, I know I spent the money and all, but I don't have a date, and now it's raining and..."

"Nonsense," his grandmother started. "This is your prom, and you're going. Your friends will be there and you'll have a good time. Just drive careful and be home at a decent hour."

They were done with dinner by 5:30, and it was still pouring. Derek looked out the window at the cemetary across the road. The rain was turning Jenny's grave into mud, and the muddy water was washing away from it in little rivulets. Why had she done it? Why had she killed herself? She said she'd go to the prom with him, and she'd lied.

Suddenly he saw something move. He jumped, rubbed his eyes and took a second look. There was nothing; the ground was still. He had to quit being so morbid. He turned purposefully away from the window and decided it was time to start getting ready.

He'd taken the longest shower of his life and then gotten out and splashed cologne all over himself. He'd even splashed some on his balls; this had turned out to be a very bad idea. He stifled a scream as he jumped back into the shower and turned the cold water on.

When he got out still feeling as if his balls had been scalded, he wondered why his grandfather had never told him not to put co- logne on your balls. Your balls stank. It made sense that if you were doing something special that meant you didn't want to stink, you might splash cologne on your balls. Would it have been too hard for him to tell him, *Hey boy don' ever splash no smellin' stuff on yer balls, it will burn like fire.*

It seemed to Derek like they left him to figure out everything the hard way. He put on more cologne, carefully avoiding his balls, and started to get dressed. The suit didn't look as good as he re- membered it looking, and he didn't look as good in it. To make matters worse, he had a zit on his nose, and when he popped it, it looked worse than it had before. He went into his sister's room and rummaged around. He found a package of rubbers, three joints and a vibrating dildo before he found her makeup. His grandmother was constantly searching his room for contraband, but it was a sure bet that she wasn't checking in here. Probably because then she couldn't act like she didn't know what Betty was doing, and she sure as hell wasn't going to be able to control her any more than she had been able to control their mama twenty years ago.

Derek managed to cover the zit successfully, then decided it would be more embarrassing if someone figured out he was wearing makeup, so he washed it off. Then decided it looked better before and put it back on, then took it off again, and an hour later finally left it on until he got downstairs ready to leave ... and wiped it off again.

He looked at the clock. It was 7:30. The rain had let up, and if he left he'd get there a little early, which would be perfect. He grabbed the keys off the dresser that set in the living room and headed for the door.

"OK! I'm out of here," he announced.

His grandmother walked out of the kitchen drying her hands. For some reason no matter what time of day, if you called his grandmother she walked out of the kitchen drying her hands on a towel. "My! Don't you look handsome," she said, clicking her tongue appreciatively. "Look, Grandpa, doesn't Derek look handsome?"

"Agh ha," the old man grunted not looking away from Beverly Hills 90210.

"Now you be careful," his grandmother said.

"I will be," he said.

"Have a good time." She kissed his cheek.

"I'll try."

His hand had just closed around the doorknob when someone knocked on the door. He jumped back so fast he damn near fell, and his hand sprung off the doorknob as if it were hot.

"Don't just stand there with your mouth hanging open for any fly ta move on in. Open the door, boy," his grandfather ordered.

Derek swallowed hard. Something in his gut was telling him not to open that door. He grabbed the handle quickly and yanked the door open before he could think about it.

There in the doorway, dripping with mud and smelling like the dead thing she was, stood Jenny Crabtree. Behind him he heard his grandmother hit the floor.

His grandfather ran to his grandmother's side, lifted her head and fanned her face. She started to come around.

"I don't know what ya'll are getting so all fired flustered about," his grandfather said. "Didn't I tell you that there was a spirit wind blowing last night? Didn't I say it blew life out of the living and into the dead? Bossy was dead; you shouldah known some dead thing would come alive."

Jenny looked at Derek who was just standing there his mouth gaping.

"Can I come in? I'm awfully cold," Jenny said.

"Agh... gee, Jenny, I don't know. I mean, you're dead and all. And you do smell all powerful bad," Derek stammered out.

"You'd smell bad, too, if you'd been rotting in the ground for two weeks," Jenny explained.

Derek looked at his grandparents. His grandmother was conscious and sitting up now.

His grandfather nodded and said, "She'd better come in and have a nice hot shower. Wash the stink of death off 'er, and she'll be fine."

Derek looked back at Jenny. "Agh... all right. Come on, I'll show you to the bathroom. My sister's got a bunch of smell good stuff in there."

When she walked in the door, the smell hit him and he damn near ralfed.

"Sorry," she said seeing that he was gagging.

He nodded, held his nose, and led her to the bathroom. When he got back his grandfather was spraying Lysol in the air, and his grandmother was already mopping the mud up off the floor. Derek flopped in a chair.

"How can this be happening?"

"The girl must have had some reason for coming back," his grandfather said thoughtfully. "Maybe she didn't kill herself after all. Her step-daddy has a record, you know."

"Or maybe she came back to go to the prom with you, Derek," his grandmother said getting that look on her face that she always got when she thought something was just *too* horribly romantic.

"Even I'm not desperate enough to take a zombie to the prom," Derek said. Then added quickly. "Not if she smells like that."

"She's alive! Got ole Bossy's life she did. Not that there was much life left in her; she was so old and sick. Girl doesn't have much time." He put down the Lysol and headed for the front door. "I better go get the drench and the pipe."

"We're not going to drench Jenny!" Derek shrieked in disbelief.

His grandfather laughed. "You got a point there, boy. She isn't a stupid cow, she'll probably drink the medicine right down. I'll just go get it then."

"And I'll go get her something nice to wear from Betty's room. A girl has to look pretty on the night of her prom." His grandmother left the mop and bucket and ran off to Betty's room.

It seemed like hours that his grandmother was in the bathroom with Jenny, while his grandfather was in the kitchen mixing the drench solution with grape juice – *So as it would be more palatable*. Derek was sitting in the living room wishing he'd wake up from the worst dream he'd ever had.

Except that it wasn't a dream.

Jenny walked into the room, and Derek stood up and looked at her in disbelief. She was clean! There was no hole in her head, and she looked absolutely gorgeous in a short blue dress that had always made Betty look even fatter than she was. And best of all... she didn't stink!

"Wow, Jenny! You look..."

"Isn't she pretty?" his grandmother said.

"Yes, very," Derek said.

His grandfather walked in then and handed the glass of yuk to Jenny. She took it and looked at it skeptically.

"Cow was sick; you better take her medicine," he said.

Jenny nodded. "I do feel a little sick to my stomach and chilled."

When she opened her mouth to speak, he could smell it... sick cow's breath. It was awful.

Jenny started drinking the concoction his grandfather had

made. From the look on her face, it tasted as bad as it looked. She finished it and handed the glass back to his grandfather.

"Now you children better hurry along. You're going to be late as it is," his grandmother said.

"Grandma... I can't show up at the prom with a dead girl. What will people say? Besides, her breath..."

"She brushed her teeth twice and gargled. It's better than it was."

"Whose toothbrush did you let her use?" Derek asked, making a face.

"Quit wasting time, boy, and take this girl to the prom," his grandfather said. "Tell them she's the girl's cousin if they ask. And here," he handed Jenny a box of tic-tacs, "use these freely, young lady."

They got into the truck, and with the tic-tac in her mouth the smell was almost tolerable.

They were silent for a long time, and then Derek asked. "Why'd you do it, Jenny? Why'd you kill yourself?"

"I didn't kill myself!" Jenny screeched. "Is that what people think?"

"Yes," Derek said simply.

"Why would I kill myself? I'm smart; I'm pretty." She smiled at him shyly. "I even had a date to go to the prom with a boy I liked."

"You... you like me?" Derek laughed nervously.

"Why would I agree to go to the prom with you if I didn't? My mother's worthless husband... he must have killed me. He was beating me up because I wouldn't give him a blow job, and he knocked me into the wall. It must have killed me."

Derek made a face.

"What, what is it?" Jenny demanded.

"That ain't exactly what killed ya, Jenny. What killed ya was a bullet wound that started in the roof of your mouth and came out the top of your head," Derek explained.

"That bastard," Jenny cursed. "And I suppose my stupid mother believes I killed myself. She believes everything that bastard tells her. He killed me and he got away with it."

"You can go to the cops tell them what really happened," Derek said.

"What? That my step dad killed me and I've come back from the dead with the life of a sick cow? I don't think so."

"Better eat another tic tac," Derek said making a face as her breath wafted up towards him.

"I've got a better plan," Jenny said. "I'll just cart my undead butt over there and kill the bastard. What's the worst they can do — kill me? Hell, I've been dead before, it just isn't that big a deal. Maybe I'll make his death look like a suicide. Type up a note... him confessing to killing me, couldn't live with himself so *Boom!* he blows his own brains out."

Derek nodded. That sounded like a good idea to him. As she ate the tik tacs her breath was becoming less offensive, and she sure did look pretty.

"Jenny, let's not think about any of that tonight. Let's just enjoy our prom, together."

She smiled. She had such a pretty smile. Bad breath, but a pretty smile.

When he walked in with Jenny on his arm and presented his tickets, fashionably late, every eye in the place was on them, and he couldn't have been any more proud if he'd brought a living girl to the prom.

Meyer, Dave and Lindsay practically ran up to them.

"Derek... Jenny?" Meyer stammered out, as white as a sheet.

Jenny stuck out her hand, and Meyer took it cautiously.

"Sorry to startle everyone. I'm Jenny's cousin, Patty, from Widows Peak. Derek and I have been friends for a long time, and I just couldn't let him come to his prom alone. I think Jenny would have wanted things this way."

"Whoosh!" Dave said, wiping his forehead with the back of his hand. "There for a minute I thought I was seeing a ghost."

The color came back into Meyer's face. He looked at Jenny with his most serious face. "I was so sorry about your cousin. She was a really nice person. I really liked her."

"Me, too," Lindsay said. She looked at Jenny's dress then.

"You know I wanted to wear a short dress, but my mother made me wear a formal. I feel so stupid."

"Well, you look great," Jenny said.

The band started to play a new song and Jenny smiled. "That's my favorite song," she said.

"Agh... would you like to dance then?" Derek asked. It was a slow dance. That meant they'd be close. Still, she looked so damn good.

"Yes, I would." Jenny popped half a dozen tic tacs in her mouth, grabbed his hand, and drug him onto the floor. Derek pulled her close, for the moment ignoring her breath.

He was on top of the world. He looked at all the geeks standing against the wall who had come stag and thanked God he wasn't one of them. She may be dead and have sick cow's breath, but at least Derek had a date for the prom.

AND THAT'S JUST THE WAY IT WAS.

I wrote this story with my best friend, Brand. Brand came to me with the idea, we sat down and worked on the first three pages together, then he got up and took off and I finished the piece. This is why Brand and I work so well together, because he comes in, gives me a twisted idea, stays just long enough that we agree on the direction the piece should go in, then leaves me alone and lets me work. Of course this can be a real bitch if we happen to be working on a barn.

Bubba grows up in a dysfunctional family.

THE STALKER
by Selina Rosen and Brand Whitlock

People are always asking me why I'm such a screwed up little fuck. I guess I could tell 'em some bullshit story 'bout how I was locked in a basement by my crazy father who was constantly talking to dead fucks and warding off demons and such.

Problem is, it would be the truth.

I remember the day I figured out that not everyone's family was like ours. I was ten years old, and we had just moved for the fourteenth time in two years. We never really lived anywhere long enough to go to school or make friends or such. See, my dad said there was some demon chasing his ass around cause of him being physic and all. So we were forced to move every few months just to keep ahead of the screwy little bugger. I really figured it had a whole lot to do with not being able to pay the rent and using up the cleaning deposit.

My dad made a living, or almost, telling people's fortunes and helpin' them speak ta dead loved ones who'd gone to the world beyond. You'd be surprised what people will pay just to hear one word from a dead loved one spoken through my dad's lips.

Sometimes Dad would scream like a fat widow woman talking in tongues at a Pentecost tent revival. He'd chase us around with a baseball bat and swat at us. Later on, when he'd calm down, mama'd ask him why he did that — tryin' ta kill the kids and all — and he'd always say, "I wasn' tryin' to kill the kids, it was that pesky demon."

Then Mama'd scream, "Ya God damn crazy piece a shit! Stop all that damn demon shit, yer ruinin' our lives."

"But Mama, the demon is real. It ain't my fault if he wants ta gobble up the souls of our children!" Daddy would scream back. Then Mama'd hit him with a broom right in the head, and he'd stagger around kind of dazed like and mama would scream, "It just ain't fatherly like — a man chasing his children 'round, trying to hit 'em with a bat. Boys are gonna come out plum warped, and the girl don' act right now."

It was always the same thing. Then we'd move to escape that dreadful demon, but Daddy was always right there with us.

Any way... We'd jus' moved to this new town. Dad was busy reuniting all the town folk with their dead loved ones and reacquainting himself with their money. Mama was gettin' in tight with the local church ladies, and I was trying desperately to make friends with the next door neighbor's pretty little daughter, Laquisha. She was real friendly, too. Always wanting to show me new and interesting things.

She had a little game she liked to play. She'd say, "What color do you think my panties are?" And before I could even guess, *Whoosh!* there went her skirt up over her head. Some days, jus' ta really fool me, she wouldn't wear no panties at all. She sure was a tricky one, that Laquisha.

One day, when we hadn't been liven there long, her mama asked me in for some lemonade. Bein' the polite and social young man that I was, I was forced to oblige.

At first Laquisha and I just sat there sipping lemonade, watching TV, and talkin' about whether Elvis was really dead or not. I said I thought I was pretty sure that he was, cause my daddy was always talking ta him, and the only important people my daddy knew were all dead.

Then her mama come in, and before you know it the weird old bitch is tellin' us two little kids everything there was ta know about her really fucked up marriage to her philandering third husband, Bill.

It turned out that Laquisha was her daughter by her second husband, Charlie, who had left under mysterious circumstances and never returned. After a few years they had presumed he was dead, and she'd married her current husband Bill.

"...That son of a bitch stays out till all hours screwing those lot lizards down at the truck plaza. Ain't I a good wife to him? I keep the house clean and his laundry done up. I even clean the shit stains out of his shorts. And this is the thanks I get. I try to set a romantic mood for him. I'm losing weight. My teeth are on order — should be in any day. And God knows I gots the prettiest wig in all of Porta. What does he need another woman for? Why I gots everything he needs right here at home."

Then she pushed her big ole titties right up in my face.

"See these? They're all mine. I don't need none of them silicone breast implants. This is all me. I'm a *real* woman."

She pulled back just before I suffocated right there in the bosom of death.

"I gots it all and a bag a chips, too. Don't ya think, boy?"

Now, being a ten year old boy I didn't really know what ta say about an ugly woman's titties. I was feeling a little queasy, so I just shook my head yes and took another drink of lemonade. Then I said kind of smoothly changed the subject like.

"Ya sure do make some fine lemonade."

Next thing I knew she was puttin' on some country western music. "I can dance, too. Want ta dance with me, Clevis?"

I got a very vivid, not too pretty, picture of being two-stepped to death right there in her bosoms.

"My mom's calling me. I gotta go."

I got up and made for the door with Laquisha right behind me screaming over and over. "Guess what color underwear I'm wearing! Can ya guess! Can ya! Can ya!"

I guess I remember that day so well because that was the day it happened.

Me an' my three brothers, ma mama, and ma sister had just set down to eat us a meal of bologna sandwiches and red koolaid when my father ran in like he had the devil on his heals. I wondered if maybe he'd had a run-in with Laquisha's mama.

He grabbed my mama in one hand and my baby brother Earl in the other. "Into the basement!" he screamed. "Into the basement!"

We all ran as fast as we could, seeing as it was tornado season and we'd just watched *Twister* fifteen times because we moved before we could turn it back in. Also it was the only tape we had.

When we had all been shoved into the basement, the door slammed. And then I heard the sound of something I don't think I'll ever forget. A big pad lock being heaved shut, and the rattle of a chain. When I looked around and didn't see Daddy, I knew somethin' wasn't right.

"Roy Dean! Roy Dean Allen!" Mama screamed. "What the hell is this shit? You let us outah here right this minute."

"It's the demon, Sally. He says he's comin' for ya. He's makin' me do things. Man's gotta protect his family, ya know. I gotta deal with this demon once and for all. On my own."

"God damn it Roy Dean, ya crazy son of ah bitch! You can't lock us up down here, we'll starve! It's wet. It stinks... There ain't no terlit."

When he didn't answer, Mama held little Earl tight and sat down on the steps to cry.

There were only two tiny little steel casement windows to let in light. They were about eight feet off the floor. There wasn't a damn thing left in the basement except a stack of blankets, a bucket, and a case of terlit paper. Obviously, Daddy'd had this planned for awhile.

I watched as the window opened and a picnic basket was lowered down with our half eaten bologna sandwiches and a thermos full of red koolaid in it.

"Clevis, come over here and get this," Daddy ordered. I walked over, but didn't move to touch the basket. "Take the basket off the hook, boy."

"Daddy!" I know it's not very manly to admit to it, but I was cryin'. "Why are ya doin' this?"

"Can't ya see," Daddy was cryin', too. "I ain't makin' it up. There's a demon, boy, and he'll try ta hurt ya. He'll try ta make me hurt ya. I gottah do this. Now just take the basket off the hook."

"Damn it, Roy Dean!" Mama screamed and cried. "Can't you see yer scarin' the hell out of the children? Let us out, Roy." She calmed down. "Let us out, and we'll get you some help."

"I don' need no help, woman!" Daddy screamed back. I could tell he was demon-fighten' mad. "Can't ya have a little faith?"

He glared down at me. "Now get the food, or ya can go hungry."

I wasn't too crazy about the idea of going hungry, so I grabbed the basket off the hook. I watched as the hook went back up. I couldn't see Daddy walk away, but I could hear it. Outside it had started to rain, and as he walked I could hear him sinking in the mud making a smushing sound as he went.

The first day we all screamed *a lot*. But if anyone heard us, they didn't help. I was the oldest, and Mama put me on her shoulders so that I could get a better look at that window. Problem being the only one who could get through the window if it was open was Earl. Mama said right quick that she was not sending her baby out there to deal with a mad man. I guessed that she was talkin' 'bout Daddy and not the demon.

The other big problem was that Daddy had rigged the windows so that they were locked on the outside. We would'ah had ta break one to get it open. If we couldn't get out, Daddy would know for sure that we was tryin'.

Mama held me up a second time, and I saw Laquisha playin' in her yard. I screamed real loud and banged on the glass. She looked up once like she thought she heard something, and I screamed even louder. This time she didn't seem to hear at all. She was playing with Bobby from down the street. I saw her play the underwear game with him and felt instantly betrayed. It was that day that I learned about the treachery of women.

As the days passed we got used to the routine of it. Once a day Daddy would come and raise the slop bucket and lower the picnic basket with bologna sandwiches and red koolaid. He'd promise us that we wouldn't be there long, that he had the demon on the ropes. Then he would haul the picnic basket back up and ship the slop bucket down below again. Then he'd close the window and be gone. At least twice a day Mama would lift me up so that I could try to get Laquisha or her mother's attention, but they never seemed to notice. And I have to admit that my heart wasn't in it. With true kid logic, I didn't want Laquisha to help us because I was mad at her.

The rest of the day we spent pretending that we were prisoners on a pirate ship, prisoners of war, or prisoners in space. We never did have very good imaginations, having spent our entire lives up to that point in front of the tube. And there just wasn't too much else to play without toys or shiny things.

I don't know how long we had been down there when it happened.

It had been raining a lot, and the walls were starting to sweat. Outside the lightning flashed, and then I heard a scream the likes of which I have never heard before or since.

Mama got a scared look, and stood up from were she'd been sitting in the floor, wrapped in a blanket. She walked towards the window and looked up. It was dark outside. "What the hell was that?" she whispered.

I just shook my head. I didn't rightly know, but I was pretty sure I didn' wanna find out, so when my mother got down so I could get on her shoulders I shook my head no.

"Come on, Clevis."

"I... I don't think we should look, Mama. Might be that demon..."

"Don' you start that shit, Clevis. You know as well as I do there ain't no friggin' demon. Now climb on."

Reluctantly I straddled my mom's neck, and she stood up. I held onto her head, and after several minutes of shifting and turning — all of which was accompanied by Mama's groaning and moaning — I was standing on her shoulders just like I had been doing twice a day for God alone knew how long. Through the rain I saw Laquisha's mother dragging something that looked like a dog or...

"Jesus Christ!" I screamed and almost fell.

"What is it, boy?" Mama asked, staggering to keep us both on her feet.

I looked again just ta make sure, and then I scampered down my mama's body like a monkey.

"What is it?" Mama screamed.

"That crazy ole bitch has killed her husband! She's barying him in the back yard in the mud." I was shacking all over. That woman whose boobs had been in my face was a cold blooded killer.

"How many times have I told you not to talk like that," Mama scolded. Then she mumbled something about how if she'd done that she wouldn't be were she was today.

I thought that was the most terrible thing I'd ever seen, but two hours later I saw worse. The door at the top of the stairs burst open, and my daddy walked in carrying the muddy corpse of the next door neighbor.

"Jesus Christ!" I screamed as my mother huddled us all into a corner as far away from my daddy as she could get.

"My God, Roy Dean! What the hell are ya doin' now! God in heaven above, have you lost all sense of reason?"

The kids was all screamin' and cryin'. Scared wittless.

"You never believed me. You never believed in me, and now I'm gonna *show* ya. For years that damn demon has tormented me, trying to get me to put him into a body he could control, like the body of one of our children. And you jus' think I'm crazy. Well, I'm about ta show ya crazy, Sally."

He lay the body gently on the floor, and then he started screaming a bunch ah gibberish. I'm thinking that while he's busy we just might have a chance to make a break for it. I whisper this to Mama and she nods, then we all start to move as one person. Suddenly she stops. I wonder why, and I look up. That fucking corpse is getting up! Next thing we know the bastard is dancing.

He looks right at my daddy and laughs, then he hisses, "I knew it. I knew you were too weak. I knew you'd eventually give in and you'd get me a body. I'm alive! I'm flesh and blood and bone. Free to roam the earth. Free to pillage, and rape, and rob. No longer a mere nuisance, a dirty little thought planted in the mind of a pious man, or a truly wicked one placed into the mind of an evil one. I'm free! Free! Free!"

There was a loud boom, and then another. At first I thought it was a loud thunder clap, then I say the demon stagger and fall. He no longer had Bill's face. He no longer had Bill's chest. Just two huge, gaping bloody holes. I looked up and saw the sawed off double barrel shotgun in my daddy's hands still smoking.

He started laughing like a lunatic. "One thing ya didn' figger on, ya son ah bitch. Anythin' *alive* kin be *killed!*"

Next morning we packed and moved again for the very last time.

AND THAT'S JUST THE WAY IT WAS.

Inspired by an installment of the Sally Jessie Rafeal show.
Need I say more?
    Bubba has an epiphany.

Surprise Reunions
by Selina Rosen

Jack turned on the TV. Since he'd lost his job at the factory, he just didn't have anything else to do. Which was, in his opinion, the only reason one would choose to watch daytime TV.

"Today on "The Suzy Show," we've got surprise family reunions... with the dead! World renown physic, Helen Cosmic, will try to put today's guests in touch with their long-lost loved ones."

"This is Janey. Janey has come here today because she desperately wants to talk to her deceased brother, James. Janey, can you tell us a little bit about your brother?"

Suzy shoved the mike into the face of an obese woman with acne who seemed to be crying real tears.

"Well, Suzy, we were very close." She sniffled loudly, and Suzy handed her a box of tissues. The she blew her nose loudly before continuing. "He died of testicular cancer a year and a half ago, and I was just wondering how he's doing, and if he can tell me where I might find Aunt Flossy's antique heirloom quilt. No one has been able to find it since he died."

"Send Helen on in," Suzy ordered. Then looking at the audience and into camera one she said, "Let's see if we can't get Janey the help she so desperately needs to put all these awful questions behind her and get on with her life."

The physic, a huge woman in a multicolored caftan, walked in with a sweep of cloth and sat down across from Janey. Jack figured that with those two beautys in the shot, the camera man had better find himself a damn good wide-angle lens.

"Have you ever meet our physic before, Janey?" Suzy asked.
"No," Janey wept.

Suzy looked at the audience. "I just wanted to make sure that everyone knows that this is not some hoax. We don't do that sort of thing on 'The Suzy Show'."

Helen Cosmic stared into Janey's tear swollen, mascara smeared eyes and said with an amazingly straight face, "I'm getting the sensation... that you are very disturbed." Helen touched her own forehead and frowned in concentration. "That you are desperately seeking contact with... a loved one."

"Oh! How did you know?" Janey cried.

"It's a woman..."

"No," Janey answered.

"You're looking to contact... a man," Helen Cosmic said.

"Yes, that's right!" Janey cried in an amazed tone.

"An uncle."

"No."

"Your father."

"My father lives in Fresno," Janey said and waved. "Hi, Dad!"

"Oh... I get the feeling... it's coming through now... you're... looking foooor... a brother!"

"Oh, my God! How could you know?" Janey cried.

"She's a physic, honey," Suzy said, and the whole audience laughed.

"His name starts with an A," Helen suggested.

"No."

"B."

"No."

"C"

"No."

"D."

She ran through the whole alphabet till she got to J, and then Janey squealed, "Oh, my God, yes! His name was..."

"No! Don't tell me; I can see it. It was... John."

"No."

"Jason."

"No."

"Jeremy."

"No."

"James."

"Oh, my God, yes!" Janey cried out. She giggled nervously. "This is kind of spooky."

"I since he died of... a disease."

"Yes!" Janey cried.

"Heart disease."

"No."

"Ulcers."

"No."

"Cancer."

"Yes!"

"He was very sick," Helen told Janey. taking her hand in a consoling way. "He was very sick for a very long time."

"Yes, he was." Janey cried.

"That's what he's telling me. That he used to be a big man, and the cancer ate him down to nothing."

"Oh! That's right! He only weighed three hundred pounds when he died!" Janey cried then added in a nervous tone. "He t... t... t... *told* ya?"

"Yes, dear. James is standing right behind you. He says he's never far away. He's always with you," the psychic said. "What do you want to say to him?"

"Is he... is he happy?"

"Oh, yes, dear. He was so sick, and now he doesn't have pain... I feel there is something else you want to ask your brother."

"I hate to bother him with it, but... Aunt Flossy's, quilt... I was wondering if he knew where it was."

"Why, he's wrapped up in it, dear! He took it with him to the other side."

"What a crock!" Jack laughed, got up and went to the kitchen to get another beer. Then he lay back down on the couch and watched the parade of idiots that filled his TV screen.

All of the other "encounters" were more or less the same as Janey's. Helen Cosmic had about as much psychic insight as Jack's half blind, crippled, mangy coon dog.

Jack marveled at the fact that there were so many stupid, desperate people in the world. You'd have to be both to buy into

Helen Cosmic's act.

Towards the end of the show the "physic" was helping people in the audience by telling them where their lost cat was and such shit. Then all of the sudden the physic stood up and pointed to a man in the audience.

"You there."

The man stood up nervously. "Who, me?"

"Yes, you. There is a very agitated ghost behind you trying to get my attention." She flopped back into her chair and convulsed for a moment . Then she glared at the man with utter contempt. When she spoke, another voice came from her lips.

"Why, Mickey? Why'd ya do it, man? I thought you were my friend. First you balled my old lady. Then you wanted everything I had, so you killed me. You took my wife and all my money, and buried me in a shallow grave under an old oak on Wilford creek. But who's got the last laugh now, Mickey? Who's got the last laugh now? I told you I'd get you, Mickey, and now I have, and that fucking whore wife of mine, too!" There was a loud burst of maniacal laughter, and then the physic seemed to come out of her trance.

For the first time in her career, Suzy was at a loss for words, and the show went to commercial without her asking for it.

Jack sat up anxiously waiting for the show to come back on. He was glued to his seat eyes transfixed on the idiot box.

After what seemed like hours the show came back on.

"What happened after the show?" Suzy's voice said. The screen showed Mickey being hauled away in cuffs. "Mickey Jackson admitted to the murder of his long time friend and business associate, Todd Farmer. Mr. farmer's body was found in a shallow grave under an oak tree on the banks of Wilford creek. Mickey Jackson admitted to having an affair with the deceased wife and said it was she and not Jackson who planned the murder of her former husband. When asked why he had done it, Jackson said only, 'I was in love, and she used me. I deserve to be punished for what I have done.'"

Jack turned off the TV and grabbed the newspaper. There just *had* to be a job out there somewhere.

AND THAT'S JUST THE WAY IT WAS.

*Also inspired by a day time talk show, which already quali-
fies it as a bubba story. Then there is the gratuitous use of tools
and Fix-a-flat.*

*While most bubbas are just good ole boys, when a bubba
goes bad it can be a pretty scary thing.*

Shur nuf!

COMPULSIVE BEHAVIORS
by Selina Rosen

Alice loaded her laundry into the back seat of her car. Then
she went back into the house and picked up another basket — this
one filled with detergent, softener, dryer sheets and a vast assortment
of anything that might be needed for the washing and drying of clothes.

Her roommate, Linda, walked over and slung the door open
with one hand, the cordless phone pressed against her ear with the
other.

"That's what I said, Janet," she looked at Alice as she scooted
past her. Shrugging, Linda shook her head and mouthed the words,
"Brain dead."

Alice smiled and hurried towards her car, threw the basket in
with the first two, and started double checking to make sure she had
everything she needed. After a moment she realized, not without
some embarrassment, that she had forgotten her purse. So she rushed
back to the house for the fourth and (she hoped) final time.

Linda was now sitting on the couch watching TV. "What
could you possibly need?" Linda laughed. "Hell, you've taken half
the house with you already."

Alice lifted her purse, a huge brocade thing, from the recliner
and slung it over her shoulder. "It's always better to be prepared. I

hate it when I need something and I don't have it."

Linda laughed. "Does that ever happen with that suitcase you call a purse?"

Alice smiled back. She'd only lived here for four months, so Linda really didn't know her very well. "Not very damn often," Alice said smugly. "Well, I'm off. Don't wait up. I may go clubbing when I'm done with my laundry. After all, it is Friday night, and you know what they say; all work and no play... and all that rot."

Linda frowned. "I still think it's a bad idea to do your laundry this late at night. And to go to a club? Well, it's just not... those girls didn't just wander off, you know. Someone took them, and..."

Alice shook her head. "Don't worry, Linda." She pulled a can of mace from her purse. "I'm ready for Mr. Psycho."

Linda wasn't very reassured. "Well, be careful."

"I will be." Alice walked out closing the door behind her. She heard Linda lock it after her. Linda was sure there was some serial killer loose on the streets of West Haven, and she was afraid to even stick her head out the door after dark.

Alice wasn't afraid. You couldn't let the bastards make you a prisoner in your own home. When you did that, they won. Besides, those girls that had gotten themselves abducted had been stupid, and Alice wasn't stupid.

At 11:00 at night she had the laundromat to herself, except for a ragged looking girl with two dirty little kids that should have been put to bed hours ago. As it was, they had eaten enough candy and soda pop since Alice arrived to assure that they wouldn't come down from their sugar highs for the next three hours. They ran through the laundromat at intervals screaming so loud Alice was sure that at any moment one of them would lose a lung. Their mother, not much more than a kid herself, sat obliviously reading an old *Inquirer*.

Alice gritted her teeth and tried to read her mystery novel, but she was starting to get really pissed off. She purposely came in this late to avoid screaming brats. After all, she had to put up with that shit all day where she worked in the children's clothing department at Wal-Mart, and she had to do it with a smile pasted on her face. The last thing she wanted to deal with after an eight hour day in Wal-Mart hell was screaming children and their complaisant mothers.

"Excuse me," Alice looked up to see the teen mother standing in front of her.

"Yes," Alice said.

"I'm out of quarters, and my clothes are almost done...." She let the sentence end there, waiting for Alice to fill in the blanks.

What the hell was wrong with people! It took only minutes to check and to double check and to be prepared. But then, she couldn't bother to remember condoms, so it wasn't too hard to believe that she couldn't remember to bring enough coins for the machines. The bitch was probably on welfare, too, which meant that she, Alice, was already paying more than her fair share. Why should she, who was always prepared, always careful, have to pay for all these careless assholes, and... The girl probably wasn't seventeen yet. She'd ruined her life before it even got started. Denying her a fistful of quarters now wasn't going to teach her a damn thing. Silently, Alice reached into her pocket, pulled out a dollar's worth of quarters and handed them to the woman.

"Thanks," she said.

"Uh huh." Alice went back to her book. *I must have a big flashing sign on my head that says "sucker." Still, the faster her clothes get dried, the sooner I can have a little peace and quiet.*

As if to taunt her, the machines her wash were in started to buzz, announcing that she must now get up and go to work. As she was putting her clothes into the dryer she saw the welfare mom slipping the quarters she had just given her into the soda pop machine. She handed one to each of the kids, and then as they screamed triumphantly, she left with her laundry.

Alice had half a mind to rip those pops out of those children's hands, tell them how really unhealthy they were and then prove it by cramming them up their dead-beat mother's ass. Instead, Alice did nothing and said nothing. Which is exactly why the filthy little bitch would do the exact same thing to someone else the next time.

It was a crappy world for nice people. It's no small wonder that seemingly normal citizens showed up at fast food restaurants with machine guns and just started killing people. It was hard to hold onto your sanity in a world where everyone seemed to be watching out for themselves and absolutely no one else. Where the stupid, the lazy, and the perverted seemed to prey on the competent, the hard working and the responsible.

She had seen him as soon as she left the laundromat with her first basket. He was sitting in the driver's seat of his black panel van at the edge of the street lights, in the shadows. Maybe he thought she didn't see him, so she pretended not to. When she came out with her last basket, he wasn't in his car anymore, and she could feel the gooseflesh as it crawled across her body. She reached into her purse and clasped hold of her mace container. Then she looked quickly around and saw no one. At her car she tried unsuccessfully to open the door while holding the mace can in her purse with one hand and her basket of clothes in the other. Finally she had to let go of the mace and open the door. She was sweating now. She all but threw the basket in the passenger side and closed the door.

She walked quickly around to get in the car. No one in sight, she was probably seeing things. There was probably no one in the van to begin with, or it was just some poor janitor. She threw her purse on the seat and moved to sit beside it. She smiled at herself. Nothing, she was thinking *too* much.

Hands, big hands, from nowhere. One on her mouth, the other on her shoulder. A smell, something funny, and then blackness.

When she first woke up her head was fuzzy. It was dark, and she was being jarred around. The air was stale smelling, and she was folded up. She could still smell the chloroform. She could hear the sound of the motor and realized where she was. She was in a trunk. For a few minutes there was panic, then she forced herself to calm down. She couldn't afford the luxury of giving into her terror; she had to keep her wits about her.

He had been driving a van, so that meant that she was probably in the trunk of her own car. If she made too much noise he would know she was awake, and if he knew she was awake that could only hurt her. Carefully she searched for and found her tool box right were it should be. She opened it slowly and pulled the pen light from the top of it. She clicked it on and started searching for her purse, but he

hadn't thrown it in here with her. It was probably still in the front seat.
This guy was an idiot! If a cop stopped him, how was he going to
explain away the purse?

She didn't have the purse, so she didn't have the mace, or
any of the other things she had in there. She turned off the light and lay
back to relax and think.

What kind of man was he? Was he after the car? No. If he
was after the car, he could have taken it while she was in the laundromat.
Or taken it and left her in the parking lot. No, this guy wanted *her*.
Maybe he wanted to rape her. Maybe he wanted to kill her. Probably he wanted to do both, and God only knew in what order.

This guy had probably taken those other women. Now he
had taken her, and unless she found some way to stop him, she was
going to wind up rotting where ever *they* were.

The car jerked as they pulled off the main road and onto the
dirt. It wouldn't be long now. These idiots never used their heads. If
they did, they'd take the extra time to drive more than three or four
miles off the main road, they'd walk more than fifty feet away from the
road, and they wouldn't bury the body in a shallow grave. You'd
think that if they were going to go to all the trouble to kill someone,
they could at least dig a good, deep grave, drop a few mothballs on
top of the corpse to confuse the dogs and keep wild animals from
smelling it and digging it up, or maybe slip the corpse into a couple of
garbage bags. How much trouble could that be? Why were psychos
so lazy?

What the hell was she doing! She was wasting time thinking
of better ways to dispose of a body, when she should be trying to
figure out how to get him before he got her.

She turned the flashlight back on and looked into the tool
box, this time looking for a weapon. A screw driver would make a
good stabbing implement. She could grab hold of his balls with the
vice grips, but that would take too much accuracy. There was a can
of Fix-a-flat, a disposable lighter, signal flares, crescent wrench, cold
tire patches, a set of sockets, nylon rope... You name it, and she
probably had it in her tool box. Plenty of things to chose from.

People liked to make fun of her because she worried so much,
because she always seemed to be preparing for the worst case sce-

nario. But you were always better off packing too much than to be missing the one thing you needed. Like the mace. In the future - if there was a future - she'd be sure to carry a can of mace in her pocket and to put one in her tool box. And just for good measure, the glove box, too.

The car started to slow down, and the road got rougher. She was getting banged around a lot. and it was getting colder. Her abductor screamed then, "Hey, little lady! You up back there?"

Alice didn't say a word. For a minute she even stopped breathing.

"Guess not. Well, no matter. I'll wake ya up for the party." He laughed then, not a pleasant sound at all. She could hear the sick perversion in his voice and knew even before he continued talking what he wanted to do to her. "You and me, we're gonna have a real good time, yes sir-re-bob. Gonna play the tunnel and the choo-choo game. You and me. In and out, in and out, over and over and over." He laughed again. Then his voice changed, taking on a troubled tone. He continued so quietly that she could barely hear him. "But Mama can't know. Mama doesn't like it when I play my games. She says it's bad to touch that dirty place. You know the dirty place, don't you, lady?" Then he screamed again, "Lady, can you hear me!"

Alice felt sick. She swallowed hard and continued with what she was doing. She was running out of time. The car was moving even slower, and because of this the trunk was starting to fill with dust. It was all she could do to keep from coughing. She found an unused grease rag and held it over her face. It helped.

The car stopped with a jolt, and the maniac started laughing. She heard the car door open, and he started singing Hank William's "Your cheating Heart." Alice flinched. The lunatic couldn't even sing.

She heard his footsteps coming closer; she prepared herself. She couldn't afford any mistakes, no room for nerves, no time for second thoughts. The moment of truth was close at hand.

She heard his hand touch the trunk. She thought he was going to open it right then, and she almost screwed the whole thing up by jumping the gun. He started banging on the trunk.

"Lady! Lady, I know you're up."   ·

Alice was silent. If she had learned anything, it was that if you

said — or in this case *didn't* say — something long enough, people
would eventually believe what you wanted them to.

He banged on the trunk louder. She had to keep her cool,
she couldn't let him rattle her, not now when she was so close.

"Lady! Lady! I'm talking to you! You God damn whore! I
know you're awake. It don las this long."

He banged, screamed, banged and screamed. This went on
for some fifteen minutes. Finally she heard it. The key twisted, the
latch released. The trunk opened quickly. All she could see were his
teeth and the whites of his eyes, but that was enough.

She moved the flash light she held between her teeth away
from where she'd hidden it against her chest and swiveled so that the
light struck him full in the face. He was momentarily blinded, and that
was all she needed. With the vice grips she quickly twisted the top
from the Fix-a-flat and sprayed it in the face of her would-be at-
tacker. Then she lit the stream with the lighter. He screamed in pain
and stumbled backwards, beating his hands against his burning face.
She jumped out of the trunk still spraying him with the make-shift
flame-thrower. He fell on the ground and started rolling.

Alice laughed as she dropped the now empty can to the ground
and pulled the rope from her pocket. "You bastards are all the same.
Sick fucking perverts with your tiny little pencil dicks."

He'd managed to put the flames out on his face and body, but
he was blind and obviously in a lot of pain. Alice kicked him hard in
the ribs with the motorcycle boots she'd worn for just this purpose.
She kicked him again then grabbed first one hand and then the other
and put them into the slip knots she had made in each end of the rope.
She pulled them tight and then tied him to the nearest tree.

He cried in pain. "What you gonna do to me?"

She laughed and kicked him again. "What were you gonna
do to me? What do you do to the women that you play *your* games
with?"

"Please, lady. Please. Mercy!"

She ran a finger over the burned flesh of his face, scraping
away several layers of burned, charred skin. She flipped it off her
finger onto the ground, as he screamed in pain. He struggled to free
his hands and could not.

She watched him with glee. His pain gave her pleasure. She dug the screwdriver into the flesh of his chest just above his heart, and his screams were ecstasy. She positioned the crescent wrench and gave the screw driver a gentle tap.

She waited for his screams to die down. "You're all the same. Stupid cocky little sons-a-bitches. You all make the same mistakes. You don't prepare properly. That's why you're so damn easy to kill. I know where you hunt, and how. I know everything about you, and you know nothing about me. You never expect that your victim is really your hunter, till it's too damn late." She drove the screwdriver home using the crescent wrench as a make-shift hammer. He let out a blood curdling scream then a satisfying gurgling sound left his lips, and he went limp.

She got her collapsible shovel out of the trunk and grabbed the box of moth balls.

Linda stumbled out of her bedroom. She smiled sleepily when she saw it was Alice, obviously relieved. She looked at the clock — it was almost two. She noticed that Alice had changed her clothes, something more suitable for club hopping than the sweats she had worn to the laundromat. "Any luck?" Linda asked.

"Nah, a few nibbles, but no real bites." Alice put her laundry basket down. "West Haven is dead. It's about time I moved on to better hunting grounds."

AND THAT'S JUST THE WAY IT WAS.

Most writers will tell you they get ideas from all kinds of places. I guess I'm no exception. My dad is constantly calling me up just to tell me funny things like, "I made casserole for dinner and your ma said if I made casserole for dinner one more time she was gonna stick me in the ole folks home. So I want you to call her and tell her that casserole is a perfectly good a nutritious meal." I got the idea for this story from one of Dad's phone calls.

Consider this a historical tribute to bubbas of the old west.

A Nose For Trouble
by Selina Rosen

Fred got off his horse and wiped the sweat from his brow with his dust covered bandanna. Then he coughed till he damn near choked. He reached down, grabbed the crotch of his dungarees, and pulled them up till they successfully wiped the sweat off his balls and inner thighs. God! he hated July - hottest fucking time of the year.

"Stupid cattle," he muttered. Then staring up at the sky at the unrelenting sun, "Stupid sun." He grabbed his canteen off his saddle horn and started to take a drink, but Lyin' Pete grabbed the canteen out of his hand. "Hey!" Fred yelled trying to grab the canteen back. The younger more agile Pete jumped back out of Fred's reach, and Fred was too tired and too hot to do anything but cuss him.

"Hey, ya half breed bastard! Give me back ma canteen fer I blow yer dam fool head off."

"Quit yer belly achin!" Pete took a drink, then handed the canteen back to Fred. "Ya ain't done nothin' but bitch since we left the ranch last week... An how many times I gotta tell ya... I ain't no God damned half breed!"

"Ya look like a damn half breed," Martin said as he rode up. He got off his horse.

"Damnit, Martin..." Pete said stepping forward and trying to make his five foot four inch frame look a little taller. "I'll kick yer ass if ya say that one more time. My ma was Cherokee, she weren't no greaser."

"That'd still make ya a half breed, dim wit," Fred said.

"Yeah, but I ain't no greaser!" Pete said hotly.

It was 1840, and the Alamo was still fresh in every Texan's mind. As such, Texans even had a deep hatred of Mexican pottery. Calling a man half Mexican was akin to slapping him in the face with a big, wet cow patty.

Fred had been with Houston at Brazos when the Texas army got their ass kicked, and he was there the day they whipped Santa Anna and made him give Texans their freedom. Fred didn't much care for Mexicans. Pete could say he wasn't a half breed all he wanted, but he sure as hell didn't *look* like no Indian Fred had ever seen.

This was only one of the reasons they called him Lyin' Pete. The boy couldn't have told the truth if you'd have made him swear on a four foot stack of Bibles. The little sawed-off runt was always running his mouth about someone who's ass he wiped or some woman he'd had.

Hell, Fred doubted there was a man alive who couldn't whip this runt, and if he'd ever had a woman, which Fred highly doubted, he'd probably had to pay for her.

They were standing in the shade of a rock out crop, and it was still hotter than hell. Too hot to fight, too hot to even argue. Fred found a chair-sized rock and sat down. He wiped the mouth of his canteen on his dust covered shirt, preferring a little Texas dust to Pete's spit. He took a long drink into his mouth ignored the grit on his teeth and swallowed. They'd lassoed and branded six calves that morning, and Fred felt like he'd already done more than a good day's work.

Martin sat down next to him. "What a time for the old bastard to decide to take a head count," he said.

Fred nodded. The old man was a stingy, greedy son of a bitch. He wanted to make sure that not even one cow wasn't accounted for. Wanted to make damn sure that not one calf was left unbranded. Of course it was absurd to think you could really ride herd on this many cattle spread out over even more land, but the old fart was bound and determined to try.

"It's stupid anyway," Pete said as he flopped on the dirt in front of them, so that there was just flat-assed no way to ignore him. "Counting cows! They move here and there. By the time you've counted this lot, some of them have moved off with some other group, and ya wind up counting them again or miss others completely."

Martin laughed. "Damn, boy! Don' let the ole man hear ya say that. We got 'im convinced we kin tell the difference between one cow an 'nother by the freckles on her ass. 'Sides, the main thing is ta brand any of the calves that have been born since spring round up."

Truth be told, Martin *could* recognize a cow by the freckles on her ass. In fact, Martin knew more about cows than any one else Fred had ever known. He could tell looking at them if they were sick, in heat, or ready to calve. Martin was all right, but Fred got sick to death of living, breathing, sleeping and talking about God damned cows. He hated to admit it, but he missed the uncertainty of war. His life had become very routine, whether they were out riding the range or back at the bunk house. *Eat*, mess with cows. *Rest*, mess with cows. *Ride*, mess with cows. *Sleep,* mess with cows. Sometimes, just to break the monotony, the old man would have them break a bunch of mustangs, which would do their damnedest to break every bone in your body. Why it was damn near enough to make him go back to his wife and four kids in Kentucky -- damn near.

He'd come to Texas under the guise of looking for a better place for his family. Truth was he was just damn tired of working in his father-in-law's livery stable and tireder still of being married and having kids to feed. He longed for adventure, so when the war with Mexico started three weeks after he crossed the Arkansas border, he found it. Lots of people died in that war, and he guessed by now his family thought he was one of them.

Sometimes he wondered what they were like, his wife, and his kids. Sometimes he thought seriously about riding back, making up some story that he'd been hurt in the war and had his memory erased and had only now remembered who he was. Fred would get just about to the point of packing his gear when he'd remember kids puking and shitting all over. Kids climbing all over him and all talking at once while his wife was screaming at him to fix some damn thing one of the little brats had broken, or calling him a slackard. She was always so disappointed in him. Why didn't he have any ambition? Why didn't he want more from life? That was why she had been so supportive when Fred had talked about going to Texas and getting himself a big spread. She thought he was finally filled with that there ambition stuff, because as she said there was a fire in his voice when he talked about it. What she didn't understand was that fire was being stoked by a big ole dose of wanting to get rid of her and her rag -not kids.

When he'd kissed her and the kids goodbye and rode out of sight, he had felt like a condemned man who'd had a noose around his neck and someone suddenly took it off and said, "Sorry we got the wrong guy." He knew right then and there that he was never going to see his family again, and he couldn't have cared less.

Except for times like these when he was tired and hot and bored sick, he never looked back. When he did think about his family like he was right now, even hot and covered with dust and cow shit, he figured he'd made the right decision. After all, he really had no commitment here. Any time he got too bored or fed up, he could always get on his horse and head for the nearest cow town. He could work at a livery a couple of weeks and then take all the money he had and spend it on cheap whiskey and whores. When he got tired of that or ran out of money -- which ever came first -- he'd hire on with another ranch and start the whole cycle over again.

Sure, it wasn't a very ambitious or responsible life, but then Fred wasn't very ambitious *or* responsible.

He looked down at the heat waves raising off the "pasture," where the cows were grazing. Pasture... what a damn joke! Stick a bunch of mangy longhorn cattle on a piece of ground covered in sage brush, tumble weeds and creosote bushes and call it a pasture. Hell! Get right up on your high horse and call it a ranch!

Fred didn't want to go back out into the heat, but...

"We still got bout fifty cows ain't accounted fer on this end of the ranch, we better ride on out toward Broken Ridge see if they is hold up there," Martin said. "We can camp in the rocks over night."

Or we can stay right here in the shade, start back for the "ranch" in the morning and tell the old man that every one of the damn cows are fine. Is the world going to end if we come in sixty, seventy head short around round up time? Hell, you have this much land and this many cows, there could be that many hiding in the brush! There ain't been word one about any cattle rustlin'. Old man just wants to make damn sure we aren't slackin', so he makes damn sure we got some work to do.

"I don't wanna go up ta Broken Ridge. I told ya, last summer when we were up there I saw spooks. Haunts or demons or worse," Lyin Pete said, looking as scared as he sounded.

Boy really was one hell of a good liar. Hell, Fred didn't want to go, either, but he wasn't coming up with ghosts or looking like he was ready to shit his pants. "So jus what the hell is worse than a demon?" Fred asked Martin as he stood up and started for his horse.

"I don' rightly know. A booger maybe." Martin laughed.

"We're safe enough then, cause the Mexican *eats* all *his* buggers," Fred said. Martin laughed and shook his head as he got up and wandered over to where his own horse was chewing on a piece of sage brush.

"God damnit ya assholes!" Pete screamed. "I ain't no damned Mexican! I hope we go up there and some big hairy demon eats yer eyes right out ha yer head!"

They found ten cows hanging around in the rocks grazing in the shade -- all branded. They also found the carcass of a cow. It was getting close to dark, so they gathered some dead fall up, started a fire, and set up camp for the night.

It was Pete's turn to cook, and he made a pot of beans that he put way too much red pepper in and served when they were still rattly. Within a few minutes they were all farting fire.

Martin walked away to take a leak, and when he came back he flagged his hand in front of his face. "Damn! If that don' keep boogers away, I don' know what would."

They all laughed, and Fred blew the biggest, loudest fart he could work up. He damn near shit his pants, but it was worth it. There was a certain satisfaction a man got from blowing a fart more vile than Satan's own breath. They laughed even louder as the vile stench filled their nostrils.

"Damn!" Martin laughed, tears coming from his eyes. "What

the hell did you put in them beans, Pete?"

"Hey, that ain't nothin' I fed him, he must ah been munching on that dead cow we saw earlier," Pete said.

Martin waved his hand in front of his face again. "Yeah, or a possum crawled up his ass an died."

They laughed still louder. Then for no apparent reason what-so-ever, Martin said, "Who do you suppose killed that cow?"

They all quit laughing.

"Hell, couldah been anything," Fred said shrugging it off. "Too damn hot. Worms, a snake bite, coyotes."

"Takes a hell of a pack of coyotes ta take down a cow," Martin said.

"Hell, it could have fallen off one ah these cliffs round here and wandered around for a few days bleeding inside till it died. It could have died of old age."

"Weren't none of that," Martin said. "Something split that cow's belly open and let its guts flop out. Looked like a knife cut ta me. Someone pulled it's eyes out and cut up it's nose. Had ta be someone with a knife."

"Hell, this heat could ah split it's belly. Vultures probably got at its eyes and its nose. Why would someone cut up a cow like that?" Fred said. He leaned over to get the coffee pot off the fire and poured his cup full. A loud fart billowed forth from his ass as he sat back down. They all laughed again, and it almost but didn't quite change the subject.

"That cow hadn't been dead long. Maybe even died today; it wasn't rotten enough fer a vulture to tear it apart. Those were fresh cuts, straight cuts, not natural," Martin said. He looked at Pete. "Could it have been some indian thing?"

"An indian would never kill somethin' an not eat it. That's the white man's way. It was a haint or a demon or somethin'. I told ya this place was bad." Pete looked around then. If he had been faking fear earlier, he wasn't now. Of course it was full dark now on a moonless, starless night. The only light in the world seemed to be coming from that camp fire.

Even Fred began to feel invisible things crawling in the dark at his back, but it wasn't anything special to this place. Just that feeling

he always got when it was darker than a coal miner's ass and someone was doing their living best to scare the shit out of you, talking
about shit they should have waited to talk about in the full light of day.

"Maybe we should strike camp, move down into the valley,"
Pete said.

"We ain't goin' nowhere idiot, it's too dark. 'Sides there
ain't nothin' in the dark ain't there in the light," Fred said.

"My mama told me that, too," Martin said. "Don' make me
feel no better now than it did then." He looked at the sky. They all
saw the lightning in the distance. "Now what the hell is that?"

"It's very scary lightning," Fred teased. "There's a storm
blowin' in. Hell, Martin, we saw the clouds rollin' in just before night
fall. If I recollect correctly, that was yer reason fer puttin up the tent.
Rain ain't evil, boys, an I fer one could use a break from all this damn
heat. We sure as hell need some rain."

"It's blowin' in awful fast," Martin said. "Awful lot of lightnin'
in it."

They could just hear the distant roll of thunder, but it was
getting louder by the minute.

"That happens out here in the summer case ya hadn' noticed."
Fred laughed. "Ya've jus spooked yourself nuts. Let's git ta bed. Ya
two girls will be fine jus as soon as the sun comes up."

They were no sooner in their tent than Fred fell asleep. Only
a few seconds later the storm hit in all it's furry.

Martin and Pete couldn't sleep. The thunder was unbearably
loud. The lighting was so bright it shown right through the walls of
their tent. The rain started leaking in on them, a little here a little there,
and they knew soon it would be as wet inside as it was out.

"How can he sleep through this?" Pete said.

"What?" Martin asked, a loud clap of thunder had wiped out
most of what Pete said.

"Fred! How can he sleep?" Pete asked.

"He's ah bastard," Martin laughed. "Nothin' ever bothers ah
bastard."

Pete laughed and so did Martin. Then there was an eardrum
piercing clap of thunder, and they weren't laughing any more. Out-

side the tethered horses were stomping and whinnying, and below them in the valley the cattle were making a ruckus. They might have blowen it off and blamed it on the storm, but something or someone had killed that cow.

In a flash of lightning, the only light in this darkness, they looked at each other. They knew what they should do, but neither was in any hurry to do it.

"We better go check on the cows. At least we ought to try ta calm the horses," Martin said, resigned.

Pete nodded. "What about Fred?" Pete asked.

"He'd jus give us shit fer waken him up. Most times he's more trouble than he's worth," Martin said.

Pete nodded in silent agreement.

They slipped into their slickers, hats and boots and walked out into the downpour. Their fire was completely out, the only light they had came from the flashes of lightning, and if they looked at each other it looked as if they were moving in slow motion. They calmed the horses, saddled them, and rode down to the valley below. The storm was getting worse, the horses were hard to control, and the cattle below were screaming and running around in a frenzy.

"What do ya suppose is down there with em?" Pete asked in a frightened voice.

Martin knew what he meant. A storm this bad might make the cattle restless, but they were in a panic. Martin was glad there were only a few head here. It shouldn't be to hard to calm them down and control them. He put his hand on his gun at his hip, *just in case*. There had to be something down there -- a mountain lion or a pack of coyotes, he hoped.

When they got to the cattle, Pete went left and Martin went right. Martin didn't see anything, and just riding among them seemed to calm the cattle down. If there was something out there, it would have been almost impossible to see. It was pitch dark, and then it was light as day, then it was dark again. With the rain pouring into his eyes it was a wonder he could see at all. He began to believe that it was just the severity of the storm that was bothering the cattle, and then Pete came screaming up to him in a panic. The thunder was so loud that Martin couldn't hear a word Pete said, but in one of the lightning flashes he saw Pete pointing up the hill at their camp. A few seconds later, Pete went tearing up the hill, and his urgency was such that Martin followed.

Pete jumped off his horse when he got back to camp and ran into the tent. By the time Martin tied both his and Pete's horses up and got in the tent, all he heard was the two men fighting.

"Stupid Beaner... Why the hell did ya wake me up? Yer drippin' water all over me."

"I told ya there was this huge bright light... I saw it from below hangin' over the camp. I thought maybe... I thought ya might be hurt, ya asshole," Pete said.

"You lyin' little piece of shit. Leave me alone, and let me sleep." Fred rolled over.

"You stupid bastard! I was tryin'..."

"Let it go," Martin patted Pete's arm. Outside the storm was passing as quickly as it had come. "Let's try to get some sleep."

By morning everything they owned was wet. They hung it all over rocks in the hopes it would dry quickly when the sun hit it. The dry earth had soaked up the water, and if it wasn't for their wet possessions and the lack of dry kindling, they wouldn't have known it had rained at all. Pete had a little trouble starting a fire, but had finally managed it.

Fred walked around the rock after having taken his morning constitutional. God! He was hungry! He couldn't remember when he'd been more famished. He stretched and walked towards camp. It was his turn to cook, and when he saw the fire was going he went right to work. He put off the coffee and put on a big pot of oatmeal.

"Ya hungry, Fred?" Martin asked with a laugh.

"Ya huh," Fred answered stirring the pot.

"Ya slept through all the excitement," Martin said. "Horses and cattle were goin' nuts. Pete an I went down to try an calm them. Pete said he saw a bright ball of light all around the camp."

"Yeah, Pete also said he laid every woman in Cowtown and beat up every man. We're talkin bout Lyin Pete here, Martin," Fred said. A damn gnat kept flying around his face; he slapped at it.

"I suppose yer right. Even so, I want ya ta cut him some

slack. He really *did* think he was savin' ya last night, and I want ya to take that into consideration. Stop with all the Mexican shit. He ain't a bad kid, and there ain't no need fer ya ta keep ridin' his ass," Martin said.

Fred slapped at the gnat again, and Martin smiled. Fred shrugged. "All right, I'll get off his back."

Pete and Martin sat and watched in amazement as Fred polished off the last of the huge amount of oatmeal he had put into his bowl. He was eating as if he had never eaten before or at least never eaten anything that tasted as good.

Later as they were packing up camp and preparing to leave, Pete whispered to Martin, "So, did ya see it?"

Martin laughed. "How the hell could ya miss it? There's like this inch-long hair hangin' out of his nose with a booger stuck to the end of it." Martin laughed harder. "He keeps slappin' at it like he thinks it's a bug."

"Should we tell him?" Pete asked.

"Yeah, in a couple of days," Martin said. They both laughed and continued their packing.

They hadn't been riding but a few minutes when Fred found that he was hungry again. He was carrying all his hard tack, and since everybody always bitched about having to eat the shit, he didn't figure they'd mind too much if he ate some of his and had to get into the general supply the pack horse was carrying.

They found a few cows here and a few there; the storm had scattered them and made them harder to find. There were a couple of calves needed branding which took up more time than normal because it was hard to get a fire going. The smell of the burning flesh made Fred all powerful hungry, and he thought seriously about trying to talk the other two into just butchering one of the calves. When they'd finished and gotten back on the trail Fred had started in on his hard tack again. By the time it was high noon he'd eaten a two-week supply of the shit, and he was still hungry.

"Let's stop and get some lunch," Martin said.

Fred swatted at the pesky gnat and swallowed hard.

They got off their horses. Fred reached in his bag and felt around as if looking. "Damn!"

"What?" Martin asked.

"I must have left my hard tack back where we camped last night," Fred said. He slapped at the gnat again and wondered where all the damn gnats had come from. He began to have a suspicion that it was the same gnat bothering him all damn day, following him where ever he went. He went to the pack horse and took out a cloth sack filled with hard tack. Another two weeks rations worth. "Are you guys having trouble with gnats?" he asked. He saw them look at each other and smile. He thought maybe they had seen him eat all his hard tack.

"Oh, yeah. They're thick today. Must be from the rain," Martin said.

That evening they camped by a small creek. When Fred went down to fill his canteen he caught his reflection in the water and saw the booger hanging out of his nose on the hair.

He looked over at Martin who was filling his own canteen. He splashed him. "Ya bastards! Couldn' tell me I had a booger hanging on a hair out the end ah ma nose."

Martin started laughing.

"Yeah, yeah." Fred laughed in spite of himself. "Real funny." He reached up, took hold of the hair and gave it a yank. The hair didn't budge, and he felt as if someone had poured fire through every vein in his body. He felt like he was going to vomit and had to fight the urge. He sat down hard and fast.

"Fred... You OK, Fred?" Martin asked kneeling beside him.

The feeling seemed to be leaving him as fast as it had come. "Yeah, yeah. I'm fine." He reached up and grabbed the offending booger again and pulled. With exactly the same reaction. Except this time he damn near passed out.

Martin was slapping him in the face with a hand covered in cold water. "Fred! Damnit, Fred. Are ya all right?"

"No, I don' reckon I am. Every time I pull on that hair... I think I'm gonna die, Martin. I don't know why... but I think I'm dyin'," Fred said.

"Pete! Pete get down here!" Martin screamed.

Pete stood up from where he'd been bent over Fred and walked away. Martin followed him.

"Well?" Martin asked.

Pete shook his head. "Didn't ya look at it?"

"I tried, but damn it, Pete, I'm blind as a bat up close. Ya know that," Martin said. "What is it?"

"Well, it ain't no booger, an it ain't no hair, I kin tell ya that." Pete just shook his head. "I told ya'll I saw somethin' over the camp last night. I don' know what that thing is, but it shouldn't ought to be there, an it's bout twice the size it was this morning. It looks like..." He just stopped.

"What! What does it look like?" Martin asked shaking him.

"Like a little egg. Like ah egg attached ta his nose by somethin' looks ah awful lot like ah umbilical cord."

"You mean you think this thing is *alive*? Like some sort of bug egg?" Martin gasped.

"Yeah, and I think it's hooked itself into Fred," Pete said. "That's why he gets so sick when he pulls on it."

"Shiiiit!" Martin exclaimed. There was a gun shot, and Martin and Pete ran in that direction, half expecting to see that Fred had killed himself. Instead they found him standing over a cow he'd shot, his knife in hand and blood all over his face, chewing like a cow with a cud.

"What in God's name are ya doin'!" Martin screamed.

"I'm hungry, man. I gottah have some meat," Fred defended.

"Key-rist! At least let us *cook* it, at least let it quit *mooin'!*" Pete cried.

"I'm sorry, pards... I don' know what's wrong with me. I'm just so... *hun*gry." He stuffed another handful of raw cow meat into his mouth and chewed it up.

Martin and Pete looked at each other and walked away. "What we gonna do, Martin?" Pete asked.

"I don' rightly know what we kin do. You think that thing... Ya think it could... Well, I don't know, be contagious? Or hatch and be somethin' jus awful?" Martin asked.

"More awful than that?" Pete said, looking back in Fred's direction. He lowered his voice to a mere whisper. "I think the only why to get rid of it is ta kill Fred."

"Well, we can't do that, not unless we got damn good reason," Martin said. "We'll watch him in shifts tonight, head towards Franklin tomorrah. Take us a good two day ride from here if we went fast, and I don' know what Fred's gonna feel up ta. One thing fer damn sure -- this is more than we kin deal with. We need a doctor... or somethin'."

Pete nodded in agreement.

They spent the whole night taking turns watching Fred, not that there was really much to see. He'd gnaw on raw cow meat for a couple of hours then walk off behind a bush and take a shit so vile the horses got spooked and the cows bellowed. About two hours before day break he finally stopped eating. He went down to the creek and washed up, then he crawled into his bedroll and fell fast asleep.

Pete was supposed to be on watch, but he had nodded off, and so nobody saw how it had grown. But it sure as hell had.

Martin and Pete awoke to the sound of Fred screaming like a banshee. It wasn't hard to see why. The thing hanging out of his nose had grown to the size of a big watermelon, and had the same shape. The shell of it was translucent, and in the murky water-like substance inside you could see something was moving. The umbilical cord now filled the whole of Fred's right nostril and looked to be actually pushing it out of shape.

"What the hell is it?" Fred screamed.

Pete knelt beside the thing and looked through it.

"What the hell is it?" Martin asked.

Pete shrugged. "Don' rightly know."

"Get it off me! Christ! Cut it off! Get rid of it. Pull it out. I don't care; jus git rid of it!" Fred screamed.

"Remember what happened before..." Martin started.

"Pull it out! Pull it out! Pull it out!" Fred screamed.

Pete looked at Martin, and then Martin looked at Pete. Neither one of them wanted to touch the damn thing. Martin went and dug his roping gloves out of his saddle bags. Pete took hold of Fred's head, and Martin took hold of the thing and started to pull. Fred immediately went into convulsions which didn't stop for several minutes after they stopped pulling.

"Ah, Christ! It hurts," Fred said.

"Now... don ya worry none, Fred. We're gonna get ya ta ah doctor. We ain't but a two day's ride from Franklin..."

"How the hell do you expect me to ride with this thing hanging out ah ma nose?" Fred cried.

They made a sling and hung it on Fred's shoulder and around his neck. Then they helped him onto the horse. He was having some trouble; he could ride, but they weren't getting any where in a hurry. There was no way they'd make Franklin in less than three days at this rate. If that thing kept growing as fast as it was, they'd need another horse just to carry it.

It got hot fast, and by noon Fred was moaning continuously. There was a small creek and a smaller tree stand, but it would give them some shade. They'd stop and rest for awhile.

Pete and Martin helped Fred off the horse. It seemed to Martin that the thing had grown and Fred had shrunk. Fred moaned as he sat down on the rock they helped him to. Martin handed him his canteen. Fred drank the whole thing straight down and held his hand out indicating he wanted more. Martin handed Fred his own canteen, and Fred drank it down as well. When he looked up at Martin, he looked haggard with black circles under his eyes and his cheeks all sunk in.

"It's killin' me. Martin. This thing... It's killin' me. There has to be somethin' ya kin do for me, man."

"It's beyond my expertise, Fred. Our only chance is to git ya ta the doctor..."

"Ya know we ain't got time for that, Martin," Fred said. "I need more water. I'm gonna go down ta the creek."

"I'll help ya." Martin helped Fred to his feet, then Fred pulled free of him.

"I want a little time ta myself," Fred said.

Martin nodded, and he and Pete watched Fred walk away.

"It's sucking him dry, Martin. He's right, ain't no damn way we'll make it ta Franklin in time. Whatever's gonna happen ta him is gonna happen out here," Pete said.

Just then a loud scream came from the direction of the creek. Pete and Martin took off running, guns pulled.

They found Fred on the ground with a bloody knife in his hand. He had obviously cut the umbilical looking thing, which had turned out to be exactly the wrong thing to do. Fred's blood pooled around the end of the umbilical, no doubt acting like a hose with a siphon.

"Christ!" Pete screamed.

Martin was pulling back bushes looking.

"What the hell ya lookin' fer?" Pete asked.

"The *thing*. Where the hell is the *thing*?" Martin screamed, real terror entering his voice.

Pete joined him in the search, and not a minute later they pulled back a bush and there he sat.

"Well... I'll be damned... It's a baby," Pete said.

"Ain't like no baby I ever seen," Martin said, leveling the gun on the tiny creature. Then it looked at him with pleading, orphaned eyes, and Martin lowered his gun. "Poor little guy." He holstered his gun, reached down and picked it up. It was still all slimy, and he realized now that it was getting pinker by the minute. He reached in his pocket, pulled out his bandanna and wiped the slime out of the baby's mouth and nose the way he'd done to hundreds of calves over the years. "Get me a string to tie off his belly button."

"Martin!" Pete said in disbelief. "That thing... It killed Fred. It sure ain't human, it's..."

"Looks ta me like Fred killed himself. As fer the other, well yer startin' ta sound like that idiot Fred. You don' go aroun' haten people jus cause they're a little different. Specially not no little harmless baby. Now go on and get me somethin'."

Pete came back with a leather thong and tied it on the cord, although it didn't look like any blood or fluid had been lost on this end. In fact, the baby didn't even look like a new born. "He is sortah cute." Pete rubbed his finger down the baby's cheek. "Still, what we gonna to do with him?"

"We're gonna to raise him. The least we kin do fer Fred is ta take care ah his baby."

By the time they got Fred buried and wrestled a cow for her milk, it was dark. The baby had eaten from the make-shift tit they had constructed from a bottle and a rag, and he now slept peacefully against Pete's chest.

"We'll have to settle down now, Martin. Get a house and such. Give him a good up bringin'," Pete said.

"Yep," Martin said laying a gentle hand on Pete's leg. "We'll get some milk cows, grow a few vegetables. I was gettin' pretty tired of this ranch hand stuff anyway."

"I feel kind of bad about Fred," Pete said.

"Don't. We did the best we knew how... Besides, it's all for the best." He glanced over at Fred's grave. "He would have made a shitty father."

AND THAT'S JUST THE WAY IT WAS.

I got the idea for this story after waking up with a particularly rotten hang over.
Bubba goes on a binge and wakes up in a strange place.

TERMINAL BREATH
By Selina Rosen

Killer breath! That's what he had. Halitosis, of the deadly variety. His mouth tasted like someone had walked across his tongue in their dirty sweat socks. The taste was accompanied by a tremendous throbbing in his head, making even the slightest of movements excruciating.

Boy! He had really tied one on last night! He spent a few moments trying to remember whether or not he'd had a good time. The last thing he remembered clearly was throwing peanut shells at the TV and cussing the Packers for fumbling the ball on the one yard line. He didn't even remember which player had committed this unforgivable act. The bartender had threatened to throw him out if he didn't stop throwing things at the TV. Feeling insulted, he had stumbled into a corner booth, and everything after that was a blur.

He grabbed his head between his hands and groaned. His teeth felt as if they were glued together, his tongue swollen to three times its normal size. He didn't dare open his eyes. The glare of the morning sun coming in the window would hit his eyes and burn a hole right in his brain. Such a hang over he had never had.

Had he over slept? Would he be late for work? He really should take a look at the clock to see what time it was. He decided against this when an attempt to roll on his side made the whole room spin, and he almost hurled.

He was cold, chilled to the bone. He was buck naked and uncovered, but when he reached for bed clothes he found none. Since the movement caused him no end of pain, and in order to find the blankets he would have to open his eyes, and his toes still weren't awake, he decided he'd rather be cold.

Someone was talking. What they were saying, he couldn't quite make out, and at that moment he really didn't give a shit.

It was probably that idiot, "Captain Morning," screaming at him from the vicinity of the clock radio. He moved an arm to shut off the radio which sat on his bedside table. He found his arm floundering in the air. No doubt the voice he was hearing was that of his loving wife, calling him a bum and telling him he'd be late for work. He reached for his pillow, so he could cover his ears and muffle her out. When he couldn't find his pillow, he got mad. Just what was this shit? No covers, no radio, no pillow. He made himself focus on the voice he was hearing, and realized there were two.

"He seems to be coming around," a soft female voice said.

"Yes. His alpha wave patterns show definite signs of activity, though they are still a little erratic," an older-sounding male voice answered. "Perhaps we should move away from the specimen."

"Good idea," the woman replied.

Jim heard two sets of foot steps moving away. Now, Jim had thought of himself in many ways, but never as a specimen. To Jim, a specimen was something the doctor asked you to make in a little bottle when you had just gone three minutes earlier, so he felt less than flattered.

Jim opened one eye slowly. When the bright lights seemed to come through his pupil and make a frontal assault on his brain, he closed it again. No sense in overworking himself. He sniffed the air experimentally and recognized the smell. He was in the damned hospital.

He tried to remember what had happened, but he came up blank. "Oh boy," he thought, "the old lady will never let me live this one down." He couldn't imagine what could have happened to him. Except for being hung over, he felt fine. He felt for his nuts, and finding everything intact, felt still more perplexed. What the hell was he doing in the hospital?

His mouth somehow got his teeth unglued, and he muttered. "Oh, man, am I fucked up."

"He spoke!" The woman's previous coolness had been replaced by excitement.

"Yeah, and I'm toilet trained, too," Jim mumbled.

"What does he mean?" The man asked the woman.

"Who knows? Perhaps nothing. There is bound to be some disorientation," the woman answered.

"Can I sit up?" Since Jim's extremities were still numb, he didn't know whether he was really hurt or not, and he didn't want to take a chance on breaking a stitch or anything.

"If you feel up to it," the man answered.

"I'm so damned hung over I don't feel like breathing." Jim swung his legs off the bed carefully, and sat up. He held his head. "Ouch!" he grimaced. He opened his eyes slowly; the light was way too bright, and he was having trouble focusing. He threw his hands in front of his face. "The light! The light!" He cried in his best Transylvanian accent. The lights were almost immediately dimmed.

"Amazing! The light seems to have some sort of strange effect of him," the man said.

As Jim's eyes started to focus he looked at the two people. They wore sterile-looking white uniforms which covered them from head to toe. It was a crying shame, because the woman had a hell of a body. She wore her black hair in one of those short punk cuts that Jim kept hoping would go out of style. The man was short, on the plump side, and completely bald. Jim looked around the plain white room. Absolutely all that was in it was the examining table he sat on.

"You've changed things a bit since I had my tonsils out," Jim said.

"Tonsils?" the man asked in a confused tone.

Jim opened his mouth, made a gurgling sound and pointed down his throat. "You know — tonsils. What the hell kind of doctor are you anyway?"

"I'm an anthropologist," he answered.

The title meant nothing to Jim. "And you don't know what tonsils are! Sheesh!" Jim scoffed.

"He had tonsils — how interesting." He looked at his colleague, and said in an excited tone. "Do you realize what this means?"

"That you are certifiably nuts," Jim said before the woman could answer. She stepped forward and tried to look down his throat as he spoke. "Better stand back, honey. I've got terminal breath," he warned her. She jumped quickly back.

"He is very disoriented. He thinks that we are food," the woman said.

The man nodded. "And what do you suppose he meant by 'terminal breath'?" the man asked. The woman shrugged. "What is this 'terminal breath'?" he asked Jim.

"Are you ill?" the woman wanted to know.

"Were you two just hatched? I've got bad breath. Haven't you ever had bad breath before?" He breathed on the man.

The man backed up, making a face. "An offensive odor came from his mouth."

"Very interesting," the woman said.

"Hey, man, if you like that, you'd probably go ape shit wild for toe jam," Jim said. It was only then that he seemed to realize that he was sitting buck naked in front of total strangers. "Oh, holy shit!" He looked around wildly for a covering, then jumped off the table and grabbed the sheet he had been sitting on and wrapped it quickly around himself.

"Interesting," the woman said, "he wants to cover himself."

"He said a prayer, and then he covered himself," the man said. "Very interesting."

Jim looked around again - nothing in the room - all white and sterile. The door slid into the wall; there were no windows. He gulped. He must be in the nut house. But why? What had he done?

"Hey! I'm not a fruit cake!" he screamed, bolting towards the door. He pounded on it and screamed. "Let me outah here!"

"Of course you're not a fruit cake, Mr. Brody. No one thinks you are a fruit cake. We are not going to eat you," the man said in a reassuring tone. "You are confused. Why don't you sit down and relax?"

"If they think I'm staying here with the rest of you crackers, they're nuts," Jim screamed. "Let me out, and I swear I'll never drink again."

"Wouldn't you get awfully thirsty?" the woman asked. She turned to the man. "He seems preoccupied with food and drink. Perhaps we should feed him."

Jim felt sick. He slumped down on the floor. "Oh God! I'm

going to spend my life without shoelaces, in the company of morons!"

"You know, Thawn, I don't believe Mr. Brody has any idea where he is, or how he got here," the woman suggested.

The man nodded. "He had been in a long time. Much longer than any of the others."

"Perhaps we should attempt to explain things to him," Thawn said. The woman nodded her agreement. "I am Thawn, and this is Jane. You are Jim Brody."

"Very good. Go to the head of the class," Jim said sarcastically.

"Do you know where you are, Mr. Brody?" Jane asked.

"In some phych ward somewhere!" Jim cried. "Where I will, no doubt, spend the rest of my days watching dust particles in streams of light."

"You are not in a sanitarium, Mr. Brody," Thawn laughed. "None of us are insane. You were part of an experiment. Don't you remember?"

"No, I don't," Jim said hotly.

"Can you remember the events of the night of January 6, 1987?" Thawn asked.

"Of course I can; that was just last night. All right, so I don't remember everything, but I remember most of it. I got drunk, and I've got the hang-over to prove it," he said. "But I sure as hell don't remember any damned experiment."

"Do you remember Dr. Preston?" Thawn asked.

The name triggered memories in Jim's aching head. He remembered him and laughed. "Funny little bald guy with thick glasses? Yeah, I remember him. He kept feeding me drinks and going on about freezing people in some kinda suspended animation..."

AND THAT'S JUST THE WAY IT WAS.

When I die they will put on my head stone, "Does not play well with others." This is one of my rare collaborations that isn't with Brand Whitlock. Bev was down for a visit and said "Let's write a story together," and so we sat down and wrote this one. Bev had three odd things she had seen in her life and had been dying to use in a story. We used all three in this one.

Guy from big city comes to small town looking for a simple life and finds more than he bargained for. Can the local bubbas save him before it's too late?

EXTREMELY ODD JOBS
by Beverly Hale and Selina Rosen

Will had moved to Buck Hollow, Texas, to get away from all the weirdness in the big city. The city was sucking his soul dry, and he just had to be somewhere where he could be in his space.

In Houston all he had done was sweat, grow stagnate and moldy like everything else. It had begun to show in his work. His stories had no passion, no life. His characters, like himself, became dull reflections of the steel and concrete trap all around him.

He needed to do something impulsive to reawaken his soul, so... He pulled out a map of the state. (He wanted to get away, but wasn't desperate enough to actually leave Texas.) He closed his eyes, dropped the felt tipped marker, and then spent the next twenty minutes trying to find the green smudge. He found it over the little town of Buck Hollow. A quick computer scan told him that Buck Hollow was a town of only eight hundred souls, and a two hour drive to the nearest metropolitan area. Far enough away to be free of the fetid swamp of the city, but close enough to dip in for a splash of culture whenever he felt the whim.

Another quick search through *Yahoo* surrendered the name of the only realtor in Mayo County. Cleatus Mackelville had a phone number, but had no web site, no E-mail, not even a fax number. Far from being appalled, Will looked at this as a propitious sign. He called immediately.

Cleatus Mackelville answered the phone with a hearty, "God damn it, Louise! I told you not to call me at work no more!"

"Sir, my name is J. Wilson Madison, the author. You might have heard of me," Will said.

"Boy, you ain't tryin' to sell me no damn magazines, are ya?" Cleatus replied.

Will was more than a little mortified to think that he could be so easily mistaken for a telephone solicitor.

"No, sir, I am not. Do you always treat potential customers in this manner? I *am* a *published* author, and I am looking to relocate to Buck Hollow."

"Son, you don' wanna move ta Buck Hollow. Ain't nothin' in Buck Hollow except a couple of cows, some cockle burrs, a half-assed Dairy King, and a bunch of old farts sittin' around on the pecker wood bench in front of the post office waitin' for the mail to come in. Which don't happen but once a week."

"That's perfect. Exactly what I'm looking for. I crave the simplicity of small town America. I need something like that to replenish my creative muse."

"Whatever you say, son," Cleatus said. "We got lots of empty houses in Buck Hollow."

"I'm looking for something with character. Preferably Victorian with a large airy room with eastern exposure that I can use for my study. It should have at least three bedrooms in case I wish to entertain friends from out of town. A small garden area would be nice."

"We got a couple of places with some fancy gingerbread on them, and every house in Buck Hollow comes with garden area," Cleatus said.

"How quaint. What about character? It's very important that the house have character."

There was silence for a minute, and then Cleatus chuckled.

"Boy, I've got just the place! Old granny Stewart's house. Got shit loads of gingerbread hanging all over it. Four bedrooms, big ole sun porch, and a garden area that covers most of the acreage.

And character! Let me tell you about character, now. This house has so much character it's oozing out of the walls."

Will swallowed hard. It sounded perfect, but way out of his price range. "What's the asking price on the house?"

"Well, I don' know. We just had it mostly painted, and it's got a good roof, and the electrical is less than five years old. I couldn't go no lower than..."

Then he quoted Will a price that was a fifth of what he would have paid for a house half the size in a bad neighborhood in Houston. Will bought the house sight unseen.

Early one Monday morning, Will and a few of his friends, all of which were sure he had gone completely crazy, loaded his worldly possessions into a rented panel truck. He tethered his Jeep to the back of it and left Houston without even one backwards glance. He was leaving the city and his old life behind. Setting out on a new adventure for parts unknown.

By two o'clock it was hot, he had learned that the air conditioning in the truck only blew more hot air, and he began to wish that he had hired a moving company. The shocks on this thing seemed to be nonexistent. This wasn't turning out to be the experience he had imagined.

Just outside Buck Hollow he saw one of the strangest things he had ever seen. A twelve foot long, three foot wide wrought iron fish skeleton. Beneath it, hanging from the lower fin, was a small hand-carved sign which read *Really odd jobs done*. Under that was an arrow with a phone number written on it, pointing up a winding red dirt road.

Will smiled. There was a story there somewhere.

About a mile after that was a four by three foot sign announcing that he was about to enter Buck Hollow, Texas, Home of the Fighting Fire Ants. The sign was faded and rusty, and Will was even more convinced that he had made the right decision.

The Dairy King looked dangerous. Paint faded and peeling. Pavement around the place had broken up, some of the bigger holes had been filled with gravel. Around the perimeter of the place hung about fifty of those sticky fly trap things, all of them filled with dead or squirming insects. There were still enough flies to form a black cloud over the dumpster. The drive-in bays had no speakers and no trays. There were two picnic tables around the place, one of which had a broken leg propped up on a rock. But the most amazing thing about this dilapidated historical sight was that the place was packed.

Will was supposed to meet Cleatus here, it being the first major land mark in Buck Hollow. He pulled in and reluctantly got out of truck. Will wound up stepping down in the middle of a mostly melted chocolate dipped ice-cream cone. He spent the next few minutes shaking his foot in the air and trying to scrap it off on the gravel.

When he looked up, a big man with a beer belly wearing a white western cut suit that would put any TV evangelist to shame was smiling down at him. Will looked from the man's rattlesnake boots to his red, acne-scared face sitting in the shade of his huge white Stetson. He had a business card in his hand which he shoved into Will's as he shook his hand up and down so enthusiastically that Will was sure he was going to pull his arm from it's socket.

"Name's Cleatus Mackelville. You must be that writer fellow," he announced.

Will didn't even bother to correct him. This time he was too busy trying to scrape the combination of business card and chocolate ice cream from his hand.

"Yes, I'm J. Wilson Madison," Will said.

"Well, you ready to take a run on over and look at that house you bought?"

"Yes, sir," Will said, unable to keep the excitement from his voice.

"Want an ice-cream or somethin' first?"

Will looked the place over once more, and making a face said, "No. I don't think so. I've already enjoyed all the ice-cream I can stand." He scraped his foot on the ground.

He followed Cleatus through town past the post office. Three old men in plaid shirts, suspenders, and belts waved and smiled as he drove by. Will waved back. They sure seemed to be a friendly bunch. Of course, if he wished to have the peace he had moved here to attain, he would have to adopt an amiable but reserved manner. Otherwise, being the only local celebrity they would swarm him and make utter nuisances of themselves.

When he followed Cleatus into the drive way of what he could only assume was his new house, he was filled with the awe and pride of ownership. The house was impressive — a real gem. A white house with dark green trim. Obviously from the Victorian era. In the immortal words of Cleatus Mackelville, it had "butt loads of ginger-bread," and it was "oozing with character." It was an accurate if somewhat rustic description.

Cleatus met him at the front gate. "Now the yard needs a little work..."

"Looks fine to me," Will said. The grass had been mowed, and there were even a couple of flower beds which actually had a couple of flowers in them.

"You ain't seen the back. See, the last folks had to leave in a hurry, and they kinda left things in the middle. Let's go through the house first."

The house needed some work, there wasn't any doubt about it, but the hardwood floors, chair railing and crown molding had been recently refinished and seemed in good repair. The walls of the entrance hall, living room, and parlor had a fresh coat of soft butter cream satin finished paint. The rest of the house, however, badly needed work. But for the price he'd paid he could afford to buy a little paint and nails.

"Now this bathroom has a little bit of a plumbing problem," Cleatus announced.

That was an understatement. The sink leaked badly and had left a huge rust stain which covered most of the bottom of the bowl. There was a bucket under the drain and it was almost full.

"The turlit has a little trouble flushing, but if ya take this here bucket..." He pulled the bucket out from under the sink. "...and pour it into the turlit like so..." He did it. "...it ought to take out even the orneriest turd."

"What about the upstairs bathroom?" Will asked.

"That don work atall!" Cleatus laughed. "But how many turlits does a man need anyway?" He popped Will on the back so hard Will almost fell over.

Will was a little upset about the plumbing problems. Still... for what he'd paid for this house, he could afford to hire a plumber.

The kitchen was a mess. The cabinets had a thick coat of filth on them, and there was no stove or refrigerator — both things he had wrongly assumed would come with the house. Still... for what he'd paid for the house, he could afford to buy a refrigerator and stove and hire someone to clean up this mess.

"Now this is the back yard, and I'm tellin' you right up front it's a God damn mess. Still, there is a garden under there somewhere, and a couple of concrete benches if they ain't been stole. If I remember right, there's a pond with a fountain out there somewhere, too. So better watch where you're walkin'."

He opened the door, and Will walked out and looked around. The weeds and shrubs were shoulder height, and it was then that he noticed that the back and west side of the house had *not* been painted. Will was momentarily overwhelmed, and Cleatus must have read the look on his face.

"Well, I did tell ya they wasn' completely done with the re-model," Cleatus said.

Will regained his composure. For the price he'd paid for this house, he supposed he could afford a painter, carpenter, plumber, brush hogger, and...

"Welcome to house ownership, boy," Cleatus said popping him on the back again. "Well, I guess that's about all the problems this house has except for the ghosts." He laughed heartily. "But then you said you wanted a house with character."

"Oh yeah, right." Will laughed back. "Shine the stupid city boy on."

"I wouldn't think of that! Well, I have to go before it gets dark. Enjoy your house." Cleatus threw him the keys and started out.

Will chased him down. "Wait a minute, Cleatus."

Cleatus stopped and turned, a look on his face that said he just knew he was in for trouble.

"You know anyone who could help me unload my truck?"

"About the only one around here who takes on stuff like that is old Harvey Don Loomis. You mighta noticed his fish sign on the way into town." Cleatus began patting down pockets. "I got his card on me somewhere." He finally pulled out a battered card case and dug through it. "Yeah, here. You call old Harve. Weird SOB, but a good worker."

When Cleatus left, Will went back inside the house to call, and realized he didn't yet have phone service. Instead of falling into despair, he unhooked the jeep and went out in search of a phone and a restaurant. Any restaurant that wasn't the Dairy King.

He was about to give up hope when on the far side of town he saw a sign advertising a place called *Wild Dick's Not Yet Famous Barbecue*. He drove for five minutes more, and he found the place. It looked clean, and he saw a sign that said "phone," so he pulled in. Inside, the place still looked clean, but was the God-awfulest architectural nightmare he had ever seen.

The local taxidermist must have gotten rich decorating this place. There had to be at least fifty stuffed animals, everything from deer to Jackalopes. It clashed badly with the large floral print on the curtains, chair seats and table cloths.

Will sat down.

The waitress hurried over with a menu. Will became aware of eyes on him and looked around to realize that the other ten customers in the restaurant were all staring at him. When he looked up they quickly looked away.

"Ain't seen you in here before. You new here?" the waitress asked with a smile.

"I just bought the old Granny Stewart place," he said.

For some reason every person in that restaurant started to chuckle.

"Did I say something funny?" Will asked.

"Just, well..." the waitress cackled. "I ain't never heard her called granny..."

"Fern!" the cook screamed from the kitchen. "Just take his order."

Fern laughed. "That's my boy friend, Billy. He's sort of jealous."

Will looked down at the menu. "I'll have the barbecued rib eye dinner, and a diet coke."

Fern wrote it down, gathered up the menu, and headed for the kitchen. Will looked around and found everyone staring at him again. It was sort of creepy. He got up and walked to the pay phone, dumped in his quarter and punched in the number.

"Hello can I help you?"

"Is this Harvey Don Loomis?"

"Yes. Folks jus' call me Harve."

"My name is J. Wilson Madison. I was told that you do odd jobs."

"That would be me," he answered.

"Well, I just bought the old Stewart house..."

"Then you'll be needing a lot of odd jobs done. I do a little bit of everything. Plumbing, electrical, paintin', yard work, fencin', water witching, brush hogging — if I can't do it, I can by God fake it."

"Well, right now I just need my rental truck unloaded." Will would wait to see what kind of job Harve did before he committed to give the man any more work.

"I'll be right over," Harve said. "I even have a dolly and a stair ramp. Never let it be said that Harvey Don Loomis doesn't have the right equipment to do the job." He laughed. "Ain't that right, honey?"

Will heard a woman giggling in the background, and then she said, "Oh, Harve! You're terrible."

"There isn't any reason to hurry. I just ordered dinner, and it will take me awhile to get home. What do you say I meet you there in about an hour?"

"I'll be there with bells on!" He hung up.

Will pulled the receiver away from his ear, looked at it, shook his head and hung up the phone.

He went back to his table and sat down to find that his coke and a glass of water were already waiting for him. The water had a red tinge to it. Will held it up and looked at it. There were little particles floating in it.

"Sorry about that, mister, but you'll soon find out that all the water in Buck Hollow looks like that. The lake turned over a year ago, and the filter plant just can't get all the red clay out. If it's any consolation, the health department says it's perfectly all right to drink,"

Fern said and plopped a plate in front of him and a basket of dinner rolls. "If you need anything, just holler."

Will put the water down and looked at his "dinner." There wasn't a green vegetable in sight. The rib eye hadn't had the fat cut off of it. The gravy was lumpier than the potatoes, and the barbecue sauce was as thick and dark as used motor oil. He wasn't sure, but he thought coca cola was probably the main ingredient. It was saccharin sweet, and there were lumps of sugar in it hard enough to crack your teeth. The rolls were hard and flavorless. In short, Will thought "Dick" had some mighty unrealistic goals for his barbecue.

Will gagged down what he could, paid and headed back to his house. His house, he smiled at the thought. He'd rented all of his adult life, now *he* had a *house*. It made him feel like a grown up.

When he pulled into *his* drive way, he saw the van. On the side of it was a painting of the huge fish the man used for a sign, and under it in small letters the same advertisement. *Really odd jobs done.*

Harve had already pulled out the stair ramp — obviously a home made job, and had it setting in position over the stairs. He was sitting on the top step on the half of the stairs not covered by the ramp. The man was tall and thin with long black hair that hung free around his head, probably he had a little Mexican blood — or maybe Indian. He was an average looking man, probably in his late thirties. He looked at Will, stood up and walked down the steps.

"You must be Mr. Madison," he said holding out his hand.

Will shook his outstretched hand, noting the wad of chewing tobacco the man had tucked in his cheek.

"Just call me Will."

"OK, Will. Let's get to work. I want to be out of here before it gets dark."

Will had never seen a man work as hard or as efficiently as Harve Loomis. The truck was unpacked and his meager furnishings in place in the house before seven. The last things they moved were Will's bedroom furniture.

"No, no, Harve. This room," Will said as Harve started to go to one of the smaller bed rooms.

"You don't want to be sleeping in that room, sir," Harve said.

"It's the room with the bathroom, and..."

"Bathroom doesn't work; it stinks," Harve said quickly.

Will nodded. He had a point there. They put his bedroom set in one of the smaller bedrooms.

"Well, it looks like that's got it," Harve said sliding the ramp into the van.

"What do I owe you?" Will asked.

"Forty dollars," Harve answered.

Will handed him an extra five. "Listen, you know my plumbing is screwed. When could you get to that?"

"Tomorrow morning first thing," Harve said.

"Great! See you tomorrow, then. Thanks a million, Harve."

Will watched him go then walked back in the house and shut and locked the door. At least the central heat and air — apparently one of the first things the last owners had installed — seemed to be working nicely.

Taking a bath was a real trip. The waitress hadn't been lying; his water was also — for lack of a better word — chunky. He did the best he could, making a mental note to have Harve install a water filter. He thought Harve was going to work out fine. He was a hard worker, seemed to know what he was doing, and his rates were more than reasonable.

He was tired, and he pulled on boxer shorts and a tee shirt, found the box with his sheets and pillows in it, and trotted upstairs with them. He made his bed, turned out the lights, and crawled in again marveling at the feeling of ownership. It was his first night in his new house. He was as tired as he ever remembered being in his life, however he wasn't falling to sleep. He sighed. He needed to get some sleep. He had a big day ahead of him tomorrow because Harve was going to be coming by to work on the plumbing, and the phone company was supposed to show up to hook up his phone.

The more he thought about how much he needed to go to sleep, the more awake he was. He didn't get it. It wasn't like he was in a strange bed. After all, this was the same bed he'd slept in every night for the last five years.

Suddenly it dawned on him. The house was too quiet; there

wasn't any street noise. He had evolved into a creature that needed loud city noise to feel secure enough to sleep. The silence was so loud it was deafening.

Suddenly he heard a loud popping noise, and then the sound of something being dragged across a floor followed by footsteps and shouts. Before he had a chance to wonder what all these things were, he had fallen fast asleep.

He woke in the morning to the sound of someone pounding on the door. He got up and stumbled over a box he didn't remember being there. He looked quickly around and saw that everything in his room had been moved including the dresser.

He ran downstairs to the door. Through the glass he could see Harve standing there wearing bibs with no shirt and carrying a huge tool box. Will was surprised to see that the door was still locked. He unlocked it and swung the door wide.

"I... I think I've been robbed!" Will screamed in excitement.

"Now, I doubt that," Harve drawled. He turned his head and sent a spit ball out into the front yard without getting so much as a speck on himself or the porch. "Ain't been a robbery in Buck Hollow since Big Ethel and Little Bill spread their rain of terror across these parts in '39." He walked in and put down his tool box.

Will ran to check the box his computer was supposed to be in. It was still there and in one piece. In fact, everything *downstairs* seemed to have been completely undisturbed.

"Well, come on up and look at this!" Will drug Harve upstairs. "See? Everything's been moved."

Harve shrugged. "Anythin' missin'?"

Will looked quickly. "Well, no... But."

"Than ya wasn't robbed. I better get ta work." Harve started downstairs and Will followed.

"But... someone was in my house. Shouldn't I report that?" Will asked.

"No offense, but why would someone come in your house, move stuff around and not take anything?"

That was a good question. Will didn't, however, have a good answer. "But my stuff was moved!"

"Check the locks on the back doors an' windows. If they're

all locked, then you must have done it yourself. People do that a lot around these parts — sleep walk I mean. I kin give ya some herb tea might help." Harve grabbed his tool box from where he'd set it down on the floor and headed for the downstairs bathroom.

Will went around and checked all the windows and the back door; they were all locked. Still, Will couldn't believe that he had walked in his sleep — he never had before. He scratched his head and walked into the bathroom where Harve had started to make a list.

"You gonna want one of them water purifyin' tanks."

"Yes," Will said. He was still a little shook up.

"Gonna need a new gas line on this water heater. I can smell a little gas, and the last thing you need is a fire..."

"Fire! Fire! Save the bird! Save the bird!" A loud voice screamed, apparently from the kitchen. Will looked quickly into the kitchen; there was nothing there.

"What the hell was that?" Will asked.

Harve laughed. "That's just the parrot."

"What parrot?" Will asked.

"Padro," Harve answered.

"Padro? I..."

"You basically are gonna have ta have all new plumbin', and that filter rig don' come cheep."

"I've got to have water I can actually drink without fear of poisoning. About this parrot..."

"My Thelma's a damn fine painter, and she could clean this God awful kitchen for ya."

"That would be great. What about the parrot?" Will asked.

"Harmless. I'd better go pick up these supplies if you want to have a working bathroom before tonight."

"Where the hell is this parrot!" Will screamed.

"He won't bother you none. Just don't say fire."

"Fire! Save the bird! Save the bird!"

Will looked all around. "Where the hell is it?"

"I'll just give Thelma a call on my cell phone, and she'll come right over."

At that moment the phone people arrived.

The day immediately got too hectic for him to worry about the strangeness that had greeted him that morning.

No sooner had he explained to the two phone company morons what he needed done than Thelma arrived. She was a pretty little woman with long black hair, bright blue eyes, and a friendly smile. She immediately started into scrubbing his filthy kitchen, and Will realized she was just as good a worker as her husband.

Will worked on unpacking his computer and turning the den into his office as the phone men installed the lines.

Harve got back from the hardware store and started working on the plumbing.

When the phone company had finished, Will first hooked up his computer and then called the nearest department store — one town over. He ordered a stove and refrigerator that were delivered just as Harve finished the downstairs bathroom, and Thelma finished cleaning the kitchen.

"I kin paint it for ya tomorrow, Mr. Will," she told him. "Right now I need ta get back and work on getting supper for when my man gets home."

"That would be fine; you did a great job. What do I owe you?" Will had a reason for wanting to pay them every day. He didn't want to get to the end of a week or two and find out that he owed them thousands of dollars. Will didn't like monetary surprises unless it was him getting more money than he had expected.

"Thirty dollars," she said.

Will handed her thirty-five.

"Why thank you, Mr. Will." She sounded genuinely excited. As she started out of the house she stopped at the bottom of the stairs and yelled up.

"I'll see you at home, Sweety!"

"I'll be done soon!" Harve yelled back.

"You be careful now, Harve. Don't stay after dark," Thelma warned.

"I won't, Mama," Harve yelled down.

Thelma left and Will went in and started to write. At about six Harve walked in. "I hate ta bother ya, Will, but I'm done."

"Wow! That's great. What do I owe you?"

"Seventy-five dollars."

Will was running low on cash, so he wrote Harve an eighty dollar check. "Can you come on in tomorrow and start finishing up the painting on the outside? In fact, could you just work on this place till it's finished?"

"Sure enough, Will. See you tomorrow then." He acted excited about the prospect of more work. He picked up the tool box and left.

Poor guy. He was a hard worker, and there probably just wasn't that much work for him around here.

Will realized he hadn't eaten all day, so he went to the kitchen to get something to eat. As soon as he walked in, he remembered that he hadn't even gone to the store yet. As luck would have it, the store was already closed, and this meant he had to decide between Dairy King and Wild Dick's Not Yet Famous Barbecue.

Now he knew the food at Dick's was bad, but as his father had always told him, *Better the devil you know than the devil you don't.* Since he had eaten at Wild Dick's and lived — something he wasn't entirely sure he would be alive to say about Dairy King in the morning — he headed out for Wild Dick's.

When he got back home, feeling only a little queasy, all the lights were off. He could have sworn he'd left the porch light on. He approached the house with caution, and was relieved to find the door locked. He opened it and tried the porch light. It worked; maybe he hadn't turned it on at all.

He looked around the living room — everything seemed to be in order. Tomorrow he would work on getting it all set up. He didn't have nearly enough furniture for this house, but that could come later.

As he went upstairs he decided to move into the master bedroom tomorrow as well. He turned the light on and walked into the master bedroom. He was almost immediately chilled. He got the feeling that there was something dark and evil in the room with him, but he shrugged it off and went over to the bathroom to check out Harve's handiwork. He turned the light on in the bathroom, and the feeling got worse. It was as if some dark shadowy hand was gripping his heart and squeezing. He was trying to tell himself how silly it was when both the lights he had just turned on went off.

He ran, stumbling through the darkness towards the door. It shut in front of him. He fumbled blindly in the darkness, finally grabbed the handle and opened the door. He jumped through, quickly closing the door behind him.

It's all just coincidence. He told himself. *It's an old house, the wiring's bad, the air unit pushed the door closed.* He leaned against the wall and tried to calm down. It was the book he was working on. He had just written a really disturbing murder scene, it had awakened his imagination, and now he was seeing everything as evil.

It was then that the groaning started. Not the groans of a tormented soul, but the distinctive groans a woman made when she was being pleasured. This sound was coming from his room. He opened the door carefully and thought he saw his bed moving. The bed springs were squeaking, and then there was nothing. He ran quickly downstairs and flopped on the couch. Just then a swirl of green color whizzed past him and seemed to linger around the banister.

"That'll cost ya extra! *Bauk!* That'll cost ya extra!" the parrot screamed.

That did it. The secret ingredient in Wild Dick's not so famous sauce wasn't Coca Cola, but cocaine. He was never eating there again, and he sure wasn't going to eat it on an empty stomach.

Everything was quiet for awhile.

"Fire!" Will shouted.

"Fire! Save the bird! Save the Bird!" the "parrot" called back.

Will started looking for the parrot.

When Harvey and Thelma got there the next morning Will looked tired

"You OK, man?" Harve asked.

"Where is that fucking bird?" Will asked.

"That bird's the least of your problems," Thelma mumbled. Harve nudged her with his elbow.

"You won't see him much. He belonged to one of the previ-ous owners. The damn things live forever," Harve said.

"And then some." Thelma giggled. Harve nudged her again.

Will went out to get groceries and rent a PO box. He stopped at the post office first. The same three older gentlemen were firmly planted on the "pecker wood" bench.

"Hello," one of them said. "My name's Jackson Powder. This here's Herman James and Max Potter. You must be that city boy what bought the old Stewart place."

He held his hand out, and Will shook it.

"That's me. I'm J. Wilson Madison. You might have heard of me."

They all looked at each other and shrugged.

"I'm an author," he said, feeling less important by the minute. "I needed some space to work in. The city is stifling."

"It's a mighty fine house." Herman giggled.

"A red light special," Jackson added. Then the lot of them just started cracking up.

"I wanted a house with character," Will said.

"With character or with *characters*?" Max laughed out through a snaggle-toothed mouth.

Will figured that was a joke about him being an author, so he laughed along with them for while.

"Well, it was nice meeting you, but I've got about a billion things to do. House needs a lot of work." Will started to go inside.

"Wait! Who ya got working for ya?" Jackson asked.

Will imagined in a town this size he already knew, but Will decided to humor the old man. "Harvey Loomis."

"Loomis is a damn good man. Good worker," Herman said.

"Yep. He kin do damn near anything. Plumbing, electrical, paint, carpentry, haying, yard work, building fence..." Jackson said.

"Exorcisms," Max interjected, and then they all started to laugh again.

Will laughed, too, and then went inside. He rented a post office box and then went shopping. The prices were insane. A woman shopping next to him suggested he go into Peabody to do his big shopping.

"Prices are better there. I only come in here when I run out of something important."

Apparently in her household things like pudding, ice-cream and moon pies were must-have items.

When he came out with his groceries and headed for his jeep, the old farts in front of the post office started chuckling again. They waved big at him as he started to drive away.

"Sleep tight! Don't let the old whores bite!" Max screamed after him.

Will couldn't quite make out what the old fart was saying.

"Silly old fucks," he mumbled as he drove. He shook his head "Nothing better to do than harass the city boy."

He made himself dinner. He wasn't much of a cook. Still, anything was better than eating God only knew what at Wild Dick's. At least his water didn't have chunks floating in it. The water filtration system had been expensive, but at least it hadn't cost him a whole lot to have it installed. For the price he had paid for the house he could afford to pay for clean water.

He had just sat down to eat when a voice cried out.

"Somethin' sure smells good!"

That damn parrot! Will spun around scanning the room. Nothing. Not so much as a feather. He'd definitely heard something, and this time he couldn't blame it on the barbecue sauce.

Disgusted, he decided to ignore it. Probably some of those goobers from the post office playing a trick on him. He wasn't going to be that easy to run off.

"*Bauk!* Somethin' sure smells good."

"That little bastard," Will hissed.

"The bastard!" the bird squawked. "He stole my pants!"

Will put some food on the corner of the table to try to entice the bird into showing himself. Then he began to eat his dinner.

He finished dinner with no further interruptions, but when he had finished doing the dishes and walked over to the table to wipe it off, the food was gone. Damn it! The bird had come out, and he had been so busy he'd missed it.

He worked for awhile, and then he started to go upstairs to

bathe and get ready for bed. Maybe tonight he would move into the master bedroom. He opened the door to the bedroom and immediately had that same eerie feeling that there was something dark and evil in the room. He made himself walk in and flip on the lights anyway. Something shoved him hard in the chest and then shut the light off.

Will jumped out of the room and slammed the door closed.

"What the hell was that?" Will muttered.

"Gottah pay if you're going to play!" the bird squawked, and this time he felt the wings as the bird flew by him in a flash of green. He reached out quickly but caught nothing.

"It's just that damned parrot!"

Still, Will bathed downstairs that night and decided he wouldn't move into the room until it was painted.

He crawled into bed, and the moans of ecstasy began. He told himself it was the house settling, but if it was, he had the sexiest house on the planet. At first he was scared, then he found that he was strangely aroused. In a few minutes he was asleep.

When he woke up the next morning everything in his room had been moved again, and he didn't think the bird was doing it.

When Harve and Thelma got there, he started to question them about the history of the house. Thelma said nothing, and Harve just started talking about what he was going to be doing to the outside of the house that day, so Will went on a quest to find the local library.

It was hard to find. When he finally found it, he saw that he had more books in his personal library. However the librarian, a woman in her mid forties who looked the part, was more than willing to tell him the history of his house.

"I've read all of your books, Mr. Madison. I just loved *The Murderer Wore Red*. That's my favorite. If I brought it by one day, would you sign it for me?"

"I'd be happy to." Finally! A person in this town with some intelligence. "You were saying about my house."

"Oh, yes. The old Stewart house. Quite a rich history that house has."

"The realtor told me it belonged to a Granny Stewart, and that she lived there with her girls. I'm suspecting they were all old maids."

Iva — that's who her name plate said she was — started cracking up. "Let me guess — Cleatus Makelville."

"That's right. Now what's so funny? Every time I talk about my house, people start laughing," Will said.

"Miss Stewart was one of the most notorious Madams in Texas. Your house, Mr. Madison, was a cat house -- a house of ill repute. Madam Stewart's *girls* were a bunch of hookers — women who lost their jobs after the war."

"A whore house!" Will exclaimed. He finally got the "red light special" joke.

"Oh, yes. The local churches tried to close it down dozens of times, but this was a cow town back then, and for all their protests the cat house stayed.

"One of the local preachers, a man named Hezikiah Johnson, had a son named Jimmy. Now, it seems that Jimmy was not as pious as his father. In fact, he was a regular at the whore house. When Hezikiah found out, he went crazy. He stormed into the house with a shotgun and killed his son and six of the girls before the parrot got him, and..."

"Parrot!" Will exclaimed.

Iva laughed. "Let me finish the story. The parrot flew right at Hezikiah's eyes, and while he was trying to get the bird off his head, Madam Stewart shot him six times in the chest with a colt forty-five. There was no trial, of course. Not even any charges. But not long after that the Madam loaded up her three remaining girls and headed out of town. They said then, and some folks *still* say that the house is haunted by the spirits of the preacher, his son, and the hookers that died there. Of course, educated persons such as ourselves don't believe such hooey."

"Of course not," Will said.

"They said that's why Stewart left. Said she couldn't stand the ghost of the preacher in her house. Guess he just kept preaching at her from the grave. Anyway, she went to Peabody and started up all over again. Rumor has it that the ole gal was still turning tricks at ninety-three."

"What happened to the parrot?" Will asked excitedly.

Iva laughed and shrugged. "I don't know. I suppose she took him with her. Every picture we have of her shows her with the bird on her shoulder; they were apparently inseparable... Wait a minute! I'll show you..."

She looked till she found a book which was -- amazingly -- titled *The History of Buck Hollow*. It wasn't a very big book, but there was a whole section in it about Madam Stewart (who was *never* called Granny) and her girls. There was even a picture of them all together with the bird.

"Can I check this out?" Will asked.

"Of course. To tell the truth, it will be the first time anyone's ever checked it out. It's a shame, because the history of Buck Hollow really is quite fascinating."

When Will got home Thelma and Harve were talking in an agitated hush. It didn't take a genius to figure out that Harve wanted Thelma to go upstairs and work, and Thelma wouldn't go. This became more apparent later on when Will realized that Thelma was working on the outside of the house while Harve was painting one of the upstairs bedrooms.

After he had paid Harve and Thelma way too little for the job they had done, he sat down to eat a sandwich. As he ate he read the section on Madam Stewart and her girls. There was a copy of the newspaper article commemorating the tragic blood bath which had occurred in his house. It was more or less just as Iva had told him, except that she had been dead wrong about the bird.

Miss Stewart's beloved Parrot, Padro, who rushed in to save his mistress and the other girls, was mortally wounded when the deranged preacher slung him into a wall prior to being shot six times by Miss Stewart.

The hair on Will's arm stood on end, and goose flesh crawled up his arm.

"Fire!" Will shouted experimentally.

"Fire! Save the bird!" Pedro cried back.

Will got on the phone immediately.

"Hello! Cleatus Makelville at your service."

"You crooked bastard! Why didn't you tell me the house you were selling me was the scene of a blood bath!" Will screamed.

Makelville laughed. "Well, boy, you said you wanted a house with character, and you can't say it doesn't have that."

"I want my money back, including everything I've put in the house to date."

Makelville laughed again. "Now, I don' know nothin' about how things go in the city, but here in Mayo County that contract you signed is legal and binding."

"There are *things* in this house," Will said.

"What sorts of *things,* Mr. Madison?" he said, knowing damn well that Will was not about to say that there were spooks in his house.

"You by God know," Will said.

Makelville just laughed and hung up the phone.

Will was screwed. He didn't have enough money left now to do anything but stay, and he wasn't anywhere close to finishing the book and his next advance. Royalties didn't do much more than pay his living expenses. Still... for the price he'd paid for this house, he supposed he could put up with a few spooks.

Harve looked at Will as he looked over the back yard. He looked worn down and haggard, with black circles under and around his eyes.

"It's beautiful," Will said with real appreciation.

"I guess we're all done here," Harve said. "If you ever need anything else done just give us a holler."

"Oh, I will be sure of that. You and Thelma do damn fine work. What do I owe you?"

"Sixty dollars," he said.

Will nodded and wrote him a check for eighty.

Harve picked up his hedge trimmer and started to go, but he stopped, turned around and looked at Will. "Will, I know yer from the big city, educated and all. But if it were me, I'd want to get rid of those damn ghosts."

Will stared at him, jaw open. "Can you do that?"

"*Sure* I can do it. I do it all the time. It's one of my specialties. But I have to tell you — it's expensive. Last people moved because they couldn't come up with the money."

Thelma who had walked out to join them, nodded her head up and down.

"Can you really get rid of them?"

"Sure can. If I can't, ya kin have yer money back."

"How much?" Will asked.

"Five thousand dollars," Harve said without missing a beat.

"Five thousand dollars! But everything else ... you've been so reasonable!"

"Hell! Any idiot can pound a nail, twist a pipe, paint or cut down brush, but how many *exorcists* do you know?"

He had a point, and the fact was he couldn't really enjoy the house with that evil thing in it. "The girls and the bird don't really bother me. I really just need the preacher gone."

"Sorry, no discount," Harve said. "Besides, the girls deserve to go on over."

Will thought about it a minute. It would clean out his bank account. Still, he was getting very little sleep, his appetite was gone, and he hadn't even tried to work in a week. "All right, all right! But can you leave the bird. I've kind of gotten attached to the bird."

"I'll see what I can do."

After he handed Harve the check, Harve insisted that Will come back to their house with them to have a good home cooked meal before the exorcism.

Harvey Loomis' yard was filled with the biggest gob of eclectic crap that Will had ever seen. Old cars, metal sculptures of farm animals dancing, and what looked to be part of a fallen Russian satellite — just to name a few items.

While they ate Harve tried to explain things to him. "See, Will, spirits get stuck here for lots of reasons. Some are bad, and some are good. Now any man who'd kill a bunch of whores, his own son, and a helpless bird is evil right down to his very core. He doesn't want to leave because he knows he's going to hell. The girls probably don't want to leave because they think that heaven is just going to be plain boring. As for the bird, who knows why he's hangin' around?"

"He likes peanut butter and jelly sandwiches," Will offered.

"That might be enough for a bird. Well, there you go. If you want to keep the bird, then when we open the portal all we got to do is put out a couple of peanut butter and jelly sandwiches for the bird."

"Why do you want to keep the bird?" Thelma asked, making a face.

"I've never had a pet before," Will answered.

Thelma stayed home, wanting no part of the "haints." Will followed Harvey up the porch stairs. It was dark now.

"You got those sandwiches?" Harvey asked.

"Yes," Will said

"Good." Harvey dumped a burlap sack of stuff out on the porch. He grabbed a beer hat with the straws sticking out of the middle, put a couple of beers in it and put it on his head.

"What the hell is that for?" Will asked.

"In case I get thirsty. Sometimes these things can go on for hours," Harve explained.

"This isn't going to work, is it?" Will asked in a harsh whisper. "You took all my money, and now you're just going to shaft me."

"Have a little faith. I told you if it don' work I'll give your money back."

He took a bag of table salt from the pile and made a line of it across the door way. "Be back in a minute." He ran around back, and when he came back the bag was empty. "Ya have to stop them getting away. Otherwise they'll just go pester someone else."

"Better them than me," Will said.

Harve pulled a faded, full color newspaper picture of a painting of Elvis out of the pile and stared at it.

"I call on the spirit of Elvis to help me gather these spirits to their rightful places and restore peace to this place here on earth. Except leave the bird, because Will likes it..."

"Elvis! Come on, man! Give me a fucking break..."

"Don't mock the spirit of Elvis. Elvis is an all-powerful spirit and more than willing to help."

For the next ten minutes Will was silent as Harve prayed over the picture of Elvis. Then he popped the tops on his two beers, put the straws in his mouth, and gathered the stuff into his arms.

"Get the door," Harve hissed through his beer.

Will got the door saying his own little mantra. "The writer has gone crazy. Lets all make money off the crazy writer."

"Shush! Go put the sandwiches on the kitchen table. That should keep the bird far enough away from the other ghosts, since they all live upstairs." It was hard to understand him through the hiss of the beer entering his mouth automatically.

Will walked in and set the two sandwiches in the middle of the table. Then he walked back into the living room. Harve motioned with a cow skull he was holding in his left hand, indicating for Will to follow him upstairs. Will complied. They both paused outside the room where the thing was.

"You made me cry when you said good bye..." A deep, unmistakable voice crooned.

"We can go in now," Harve said.

Will walked in the room with Harve and the spirit of Elvis. The thing inside was mad immediately, and it hit Harve hard enough to knock the straws out of his mouth.

Beer went everywhere.

It shoved past Will, and Will caught a brief image of a man wearing black. Harve got up and ran past him. He threw the cow's skull in the direction of the fleeing spirit, and it screamed out and vanished. Next thing Will knew, the cow skull was coming straight at him. Harve stepped in front of him, a baseball bat in hand, and smashed the skull towards the room. There was a swirl of light in the room followed by darkness. Without asking, Will knew the evil presence was gone from his home.

The next thing he saw was The King walking out of his bedroom with six women hanging all over him.

"You'll see, girls. The other side is one big party." He marched them into the light, and then all was still.

"Thanks, Elvis," Harve said. He had the straws back in his mouth again.

"That... that was it?" Will asked in disbelief.

"Hey! I told ya I was good. Tomorrow Thelma will come by and clean up any mess that's left over. Consider it part of the service.

Will flopped on the couch feeling all done in. Almost immediately he felt a slight pressure on his shoulder.

"Hey, soldier! Show you a good time?" the bird squawked.

Will laughed. So he'd had to pay five thousand dollars for an exorcism. Still... with the price he'd paid for the house...

He'd been hosed.

AND THAT'S JUST THE WAY IT WAS.

*For about two years I worked in a pallet mill running an
industrial plane. The saw described in this story was in the mill
where I worked, and I think when you read about it you'll see
why I felt compelled to write about it. While there I also worked
with a guy just like Herman. It's sad, but it's true.*

Bubba has a really cool tool and a bad home life.

GANG RIPPED
by Selina Rosen

Tester, it was a town where dreams went to die.

There wasn't much to it. A post office, general store, the
cafe, three churches and the park. Blink your eyes doing fifty, and
you could miss the whole damn thing.

The inhabitants were not nearly so interesting. For the most
part, they were a bunch of white-trash crackers whose lives consisted
of trying to find new and interesting ways to waste their welfare checks.
The biggest majority of them stayed drunk, high, or both most of the
time. Except on Sunday when at least half of them attended one of
the three churches and prayed for all the sinning bastards who weren't
in church and hadn't been saved.

If you wanted to stand out in Tester, all you had to do was go
to work. These few rebellious souls had only three options. First,
they could commute to the city — an eighty minute drive in good
weather. Their second choice was to work in the log woods. Or
third, they could work at the pallet mill. The pallet mill was Tester's
leading industry. It was Tester's *only* industry.

It was far from the greatest place on Earth, but it was home to
Max.

Most would say there was so much noise you couldn't hear
yourself think. Max put in his ear plugs and enjoyed the peace all that
noise afforded him. Even with the plugs in, he could hear the machinery buzzing, clanging and ripping all around him. But for Max, the

sounds were soothing. A kind of loud quiet in which nothing could interrupt his thoughts.

The noise successfully made attempts at conversation impossible. Max wasn't particularly antisocial, but solitude was something he was having more and more trouble finding these days. Besides which, he could have a more intelligent conversation with broccoli than one of his coworkers.

Max had problems. He needed to think, and he just couldn't do that at home anymore. Which was, of course, his main problem. For Max, work was a temporary reprieve from all that was wrong with his personal life. In fact, there was only one thing that kept his job from being perfect.

"Hey Maxi! How ya doin'?"

The voice was slurred and cut through even the noise and ear plugs. The breath was the breath of a man who hadn't brushed his teeth in over two weeks, and who'd had too much cheap beer the night before.

Herman! God, how he hated Herman. He couldn't remember a time when Herman hadn't showed up for work drunk, hungover, or both. Anywhere else in the world, the man would have been canned long ago. But in Tester, the fact that he showed up at all made him a valued employee.

It wasn't the fact that Herman was a filthy, slovenly, drunk that put Max's teeth on edge, although it sure didn't help. There was just something *wrong* with the guy. There was a vacant look in his washed out blue eyes, and the way he looked at *very* young little girls was enough to creep anyone out.

Herman was the only "human" Max knew who had consumed antifreeze and lived to brag about it. Herman was what your mother threatened you would turn into if you didn't eat your spinach. Herman was the reason that cousins shouldn't marry. In short, Herman was about as far away from being human as you could get and still have a driver's license.

Herman got closer and screamed louder. "Hey Maxi! How ya doin'?"

Max was hit with the full force of the creep's breath.

"Fine, Herman," Max grated out. He suppressed the desire

to grab Herman by the throat and throttle him by reminding himself that he would have to touch him. Happily, Herman wasn't going to stick around and try to talk to him today. For once, he appeared to be going somewhere so he could pretend to be working. Max wasn't really sure what job Herman was supposed to do at the mill, but it was a sure bet that he wasn't doing it.

"Stupid old shithead." Max didn't even bother to lower his voice. After all, no one could hear him, and he didn't really care if they did.

For the next few minutes, Max concentrated on running his machine. He loved his saw. To him, running it was as exciting as flying a jet or driving a race car. It was that same kind of power. Or at least Max imagined that it was.

They called it the gang rip, and it was a thing of beauty – a huge green box with an opening in each end. Max pushed forty-inch long, five-inch thick cants* in one side, and one by sixes came out the other. It held twelve twenty-inch carbide-tipped blades that chewed through hardwood as if it were eating oatmeal. Max pushed the cants over the metal rollers till the metal track bit into the wood. The track was covered with sharp metal teeth that held the wood as the track pulled it through. Once a cant was in those teeth, there was no chance of its being thrown back at the operator. In fact, if for some reason you had to get a log out, you had to reverse the machine. Most of the time reverse wouldn't work, so you tried not to get one in there crooked. Essentially, once something was in the gang rip, it was there to stay – till it came out in pieces.

It was an awesome machine of great power, and Max always treated it with great respect. He was all too aware of how dangerous the gang rip was. If you got a hand caught between a cant and the metal teeth, it would pull you right into the blades because once caught, you couldn't reach the control buttons. Even if someone else heard your cries for help over all the noise and could get to the controls in time, you'd probably still lose a hand.

Max wasn't worried, just cautious. The machine was set up so that you would have to put your hand into it to get caught, and there was just no good reason to do that.

Logs already sawn on two sides

The day moved ever forward till it was 4:30. Quitting time. Max didn't share his co-workers' enthusiasm. He clocked out, declined the offer of his co-workers to join them for a beer in the park, jumped on his dirt bike and headed for home. Mary had said she was going shopping, and with any luck she wouldn't be home yet.

No such luck.

When he pulled into the driveway, her car was already sitting there. He slowed the bike considerably, and wondered fleetingly if he shouldn't reconsider the offer his co-workers had made. In the end, he drove on in and turned the bike off.

He sighed and just sat there. It was all his fault. He had married the bitch. He couldn't really remember why now, but he had a hunch that it had something to do with wanting frequent sex and someone to do his laundry.

"Why expect the worst, Max?" he asked himself. "You might walk in and she won't have it on. She might even have cooked dinner, and everything will be cool." Getting off the bike, he looked fleetingly over at his pickup. If he had the alternator he could just go put it in. Unfortunately, the part wouldn't come in for another two days. Of course, Mary didn't know that. He could just stay out here and pretend to fiddle with it till it was time to go to bed. But why prolong the inevitable? He took a deep breath and walked into the house.

As he stepped in the front door he ran his hand through his hair and gritted his teeth in frustration. Some fucking talk show on the TV, and the smell of a filthy cat box heavy in the air. He flopped down in the first chair he came to and sighed again.

She was laying there like some huge beached whale sucking down sour cream and onion flavored potato chips like a fucking vacuum. There were two open containers of Little Debbie snack cakes on the counter.

When he had married her she had been a cute little brunette with a body to kill for. Within three years she had blossomed into a three-hundred-fifty-pound bleach-blond slug, whose greatest ambition in life seemed to be to make his life a living hell.

When they had first married all he wanted was to have a couple of kids and make a nice life for them and Mary. But as Mary grew in size and attitude, Max began to be happy that whatever wasn't work-ing, *wasn't* working, and that he and Mary had remained childless. Of course it helped that they hadn't had sex in over a year.

She hadn't just let her body go. He could have handled the weight. She had let *everything* go. She didn't keep herself clean, she wouldn't clean house, or do the laundry. The only reason she cooked was so she could eat. It seemed like he had married this sweet wonderful woman on Saturday, and by Monday she was a raging, screaming swamp-thing.

"You go shopping?" Max asked.

"Yeah," she answered neither stopping her potato chip munch-ing or turning away from the drama of the woman who had learned she had married her own brother.

"Did you fix dinner yet?"

"No. I was to tired from shopping. There's plenty to eat, fix yourself something," she said. A hint of anger entered her voice, as if it was a hell of a lot that he ask her to shop and cook dinner in the same day.

"I've been working all day, Mary," Max said sharply. "I need more than some oatmeal pies and a fist full of chips to sustain me."

"Maybe if you got a *real* job we could afford something else," she snapped back.

That was it. That was all he fucking needed. "What about the fucking cat box. Some reason you couldn't get off your fat ass and clean that mother fucker?"

He jumped out of the chair, went in the bathroom and grabbed up the cat box full of shit. He opened the door and slung cat box and all out.

"Well, that's real cute," Mary said still not bothering to quit eating or to look away from the TV. "Now what are we supposed to do for a cat box?"

"We don't need a fucking cat box, because we ain't going to have no fucking cats!" Max ran around the house till he had found both cats sleeping in the middle of their bed. He grabbed one in each hand and went to the front door and slung them out, too. They flew through the night screaming all the way, and Mary finally quit eating.

She got to her feet and screamed at the top of her lungs. "You bastard! How could you do that? They have never been ouside!" She pushed him as she waddled towards the door.

"Hey! I have to do every fucking thing around here. I ain't changing that fucking litter box even one more time. I don't even *like* cats."

"Here kitty, kitty!" Mary shrilled into the night.

"Those cats aren't coming back in this house," Max said with determination. "You never clean the fucking cat box, and then they shit in my fucking shoes. I've just had it. In fact, I've had it with everything. I'm tired of being married to a big-lard assed bitch. What the hell do I get out of this marriage? You won't work. You don't clean house. You don't even keep your*self* clean. You never talk to me because you're always too damn busy watching the fucking boob tube. You are a fucking bitch, and I want you and your fucking cats out of my life and out of my house."

She turned to look at him then with the most hateful look he had ever seen. Tears rolling down her fat checks. "Well, then you're in a hell of a fix asshole, because this here's a community property state, and yer gonna have ta sell this little shit-ass hill farm yer daddy built with his own two hands and give me half the money."

Max left without really being aware that he had done so. The cool spring breeze hit his face. The air was fragrant with the smell of flowers in bloom, and he felt like his whole world had just imploded.

He didn't really have anywhere to go, and he wasn't too surprised when he wound up at the mill. He turned the headlights off, killed the ignition, and let the bike coast into the mill yard where he hid the bike behind one of the buildings. Not because he planned to do anything wrong, but because he didn't want to get blamed if someone else did.

It wasn't the first time Max had come here to hide from life and Mary. He'd never had any trouble finding his way into the building. Even with the doors bolted, there had to be a dozen spots where even a very big man could get in. It was small wonder that they had so much trouble with thefts.

Tonight Max sought entrance through the shaker-conveyer. It ran under all the major saws, carrying out whatever dust the blowers couldn't handle, and all the heavy wood pieces that fell from the various saws. It would have been a major engineering feat to make a door to close it up when they weren't operating, so they had never bothered.

Max crawled through the exit and stayed on his hands and knees till he reached a spot where he could crawl up into the mill. He hauled himself up out of the shaker, and sighed with relief. Now he could relax. Maybe here alone he could figure out what to do about Mary. God, what a mess things had become!

But just when he was about to get down to some real serious thinking, he heard a noise and the lights came on. He looked up, startled by the sudden intrusion. When he saw who had disturbed him, he cringed. Damn! What luck! He would have rather it been the cops. This was the last person on earth that he wanted to see.

Herman!

"Ah, Maxi, what ya doin'?" His voice was slurred, and he was listing to one side. He wasn't just drunk, he was shit-faced drunk.

"Eat shit and die," Max said hotly.

"Don' worry, Maxi. I won' tell no one it's you what's been stealin' the tools." Herman staggered and almost fell.

"I haven't stolen anything, you drunken fool." Max was not in the mood for subtleties. "No doubt you've been stealing them so that you could buy Nyquil, or whatever the hell kind of cough medicine it is that you drink these days. You've got no more right to be here than I have."

Herman laughed the laugh of the inebriated. Which is to say that no one — including Herman — knew why he was laughing. He stopped as abruptly as he had started.

"Give me a ten spot till payday, Maxi."

It was Max's turn to laugh. "I wouldn't give you the sweat of my balls if you were dying of thirst."

"I'll tell them it's you that's been stealin' the tools." Herman's threat was slurred, but clearly he thought it would work.

"Go away, Herman," Max said shortly. He hated Herman at most times, but in the mood he was in he wasn't about to put up with this old drunk's shit. "I mean it, Herman. Go away and leave me alone."

But he didn't go away. He just stood there, rattling on and on.

"Go away, Herman," Max said with a hiss. Max got up and started turning on machinery. He wasn't worried about the noise alerting anyone. The mill was quite a ways from town, and with the party raging at the park it wasn't likely that anyone would have heard anyway.

First he turned on the shaker conveyer, but he could still hear Herman. So he turned on the blowers. Herman just screamed louder. So Max turned on the gang rip.

Herman was not to be put down that easily. He got right up in Max's face, breathing his vile breath right up Max's nose.

"I'm gonna tell 'em, Maxi! If you don' give me ten bucks, I'm gonna tell 'em ya stole the tools. Ya better listen to me, Maxi..."

Max snapped. He grabbed Herman and threw him on the rollers that led to the gang rip. Herman's feet caught in the steel toothed tracks that fed the twelve hungry blades. He screamed, and Max realized what he was doing. He hit the button that stopped the tracks.

Max looked at Herman. Herman was trapped. His feet were stuck just a fraction of an inch away from the humming blades. He must be in a great deal of pain. He must be scared shitless.

It was the first time Max had ever seen Herman completely sober.

Herman's eyes were full of fear. He looked at Max in panic, mutely pleading for help.

Max looked at the scene with a sort of detached interest. He felt quite sane for the first time in weeks.

"What the hell ya doin', man? Come on, Maxi, get me outtah this," Herman pleaded.

Max smiled a sadistic smile. "My name is Max. It's not Maxamillion. Not Maxine. *Not Maxi!* My name is *Max.* M.A.X., Max!" He turned the feed on forward.

Herman let out one long blood-curdling scream as his body was pulled into the blades. He didn't stop screaming till the blades hit his midsection. Max wondered fleetingly if he was dead already or just unconscious. Before he could speculate further, all that was left of Herman disappeared into the gang rip. He ran around to the end of the saw. Morbid curiosity. He wanted to see what came out the other end.

It wasn't anything that was recognizable as having once been human. Since it wasn't stiff — the consistency of spaghetti, in fact — it slipped through the six inch gap between the end of the gang rip and the slat conveyer that usually carried the finished wood off to where it was stacked.

He watched it as it oozed out and fell in pieces into the shaker conveyer. Was that a piece of cloth, of bone, of brain, of hair? Was that an ear? Max couldn't be sure. What came out wasn't pretty, but it wasn't all that gross, either.

The gang rip had reduced Herman to a pile of bloody-looking gore which was slipping and slushing its way out of the building courtesy of the shaker conveyer.

Max looked around. He would have expected blood. Lots of blood everywhere. But the industrial blowers which were used to carrying away tons of damp sawdust hadn't had any trouble with Herman. They hummed, now obviously empty, as if to say "What's a little blood and a few bone fragments?"

There was a little blood on the slat conveyer, and he was sure that the gang rip was a mess. He got a vision of an eyeball hanging between the blades, and only then seemed to realize what he had done.

God! What have I done? I'm a murderer! I've killed a human being... No, I haven't. I've killed Herman. More like stepping on a bug.

No excuse! He had killed a man, a living, breathing man and what a horrible death!

Herman had been a living, breathing hemorrhoid. The world was better off without him. At least the death, while grizzly had been quick.

But he was going to go to jail. He was going to fry for doing the community a public service. He looked at the blood. Then he saw the hose. Using it, he cleaned the blood off the slat conveyer, and then he hosed out the gang rip. He let the water run long after he thought it was clean. The water ran into the shaker conveyer, cleaning it at the same time. When done, he put the hose back where he had found it.

No trace!

He smiled with satisfaction. No trace. The blood and bone fragments would have been carried up into the dust trailer — a semi trailer connected to the end of the blower pipe that was taken away when full and replaced — no one was going to check in there. Even if they did, the tannic acid in the oak would discolor the blood so that it couldn't be recognized. As for the bigger pieces of Herman. Well, there were always a dozen or more stray dogs hanging around the mill, and they were always hungry. Even now, Max could hear them fighting over Herman's remains. Max had been wrong about Herman; it turned out he was good for something after all.

He shut everything down and doused the lights. For obvious reasons, he chose not to exit the way he had come in; he went out a window instead.

He sweat bullets until he had pushed the bike back up to the road. The party was still raging in the park. If anyone had heard anything, they were choosing to ignore it. He started the bike and headed for home.

Max knew he should be horrified by what he had done, but he just wasn't. He had felt worse about deer he had killed hunting. He had killed Herman, and he was going to get away with it because no one would even worry about where Herman was. They would figure that he was off on a drunk. When he didn't show up after a few weeks, his wife would throw a party and every one would say, "Hey! Whatever happened to ole Herman?" A few fools would make up an answer, and only he would know the truth.

No one would care.

Max walked into the house. She was laying up in the big middle of the couch with both cats watching yet another damned talk show.

Max smiled his new smile.

"Mary," he said sweetly. "I'm sorry I yelled at you, and I'm sorry about throwing the cats outside. That was really over the top. You're right, I am an asshole. Come on, let's go for a ride. I want to show you something. You'll never believe what Herman's doing now."

Max woke up alone. He stretched. The morning air smelled sweet. It was a new day.

Tester. It wasn't such a bad little place after all.

AND THAT'S JUST THE WAY IT WAS.

This story was inspired, unfortunately, by a true event. When you write, you can change the real outcome of a story and make the world just. In real life, rich, influential people get away with everything including murder, and poor people eat shit.
Teen bubbas band together to help a friend in need.

TJ's Revenge
by Selina Rosen

"You're shitting me!" Amy screamed into the phone. She slammed on her brakes just short of running the stop sign. "That bastard! He can't do that to me! I'll get him! I'll get him good.... I'm going there right now."

She didn't bother to look, or if she did, she only did a half-assed job. She was in a hurry, and nothing obvious was in her way. She pulled her foot off the brake and slammed it down on the accelerator. The car took off with a gravel-spinning lurch and zoomed into the intersection. She was still on the phone and not really paying attention to anything but getting where she wanted to be.

Suddenly there he was. Amy freaked completely out. She didn't even remember to hit her brakes, so she plowed right into the motor bike and its rider. The rider was thrown off the bike and landed in the suicide lane. The bike disappeared under her car. The car skidded for about three more feet, then the engine struggled and died. Her front tires were resting on both of the bike's wheels, so that the front of her car was now considerably higher than the back. For a second, it was as if the whole world had stopped. As if somehow everyone was as surprised by what had happened as she was. Then the night erupted with sound -- people screaming, horns blaring, cars skidding to a stop.

Amy looked at the phone in her hand. Suzy's voice was screaming, "Amy, what happened? Amy? Amy? Can you hear me?"

"Suzy, I'll get back to you. There's been a little accident."

She turned the phone off.

"Man... You're not listening, officer. I said I *saw* her. She was on the phone!" Bug Man screamed as he stood over the crumpled body of his injured friend. TJ was conscious, but in a lot of pain, and his right leg was laying at all sorts of angles it shouldn't have been able to.

The officer looked over at the girl still sitting in her car. She hadn't bothered to get out yet. Not even to see how the kid was doing. They had taken her statement through the window. They didn't even make her get out to take a sobriety check, which was more or less SOP in any other wreck. She had been on the phone when they pulled up. She was on the phone right now, and it looked like she was having a casual conversation with a friend. That's how rattled the *poor* girl was. Still, he knew where his loyalty had to lay. It wasn't fair, but then damn few things in life were, and the boy might as well learn that now.

"She smacked right into him," Derek, another of TJ's friends, said accusingly. "I saw the whole thing. Bug Man and I were sitting right there in the patio at Taco Bell."

TJ's parents got there before the ambulance did. His mother ran towards him, and the cops tried to stop her. "That's my son!" she cried, and they grudgingly let her through.

TJ's father was right behind her.

Charlotte knelt beside her son. "TJ!" she cried. "TJ, can you hear me?"

"I'll be OK mom," TJ managed.

The ambulance pulled up. As they started to work on ,TJ, Charlotte, stood up. She looked at the girl still sitting in the car, talking on the phone. "Look at that fucking little bitch. I'm gonna kick her God damned snooty little ass!" She started forward and the cops stopped her.

"Ma'am, calm down now," the officer said.

"Calm down! That bitch just ran over my son!" Charlotte screamed.

Her husband put a hand on her shoulder. "Charlotte, go with TJ to the hospital. I'll follow you in our car."

"But look at her! She's just sitting there like nothing happened," Charlotte said. She was crying. She was scared to death
and mad as hell. But Charlotte got into the ambulance as they loaded
her son. The EMT guys were telling her that TJ was going to be fine,
but since she knew they'd say that no matter what, it really wasn't
very comforting. She felt helpless. Up till this moment, she had always had the power to take care of anything that happened to TJ, but
this was beyond her capabilities. This couldn't be fixed with a kiss
and a bandage.

As soon as the ambulance was out of sight, Tom walked up
to the cop. "It's one of those fucking Ashe kids, isn't it?" he cussed.

The cop gave him his best warning look. "Now, sir, there
isn't no need to talk like that..."

"That bitch just ran over my only son! I'll talk any way I
damn well please," Tom said in disbelief. On a big, healthy strapping
guy maybe the look and the tone of his voice might have been enough
to intimidated Tom -- maybe. This short, fat, donut-eating reject sure
as hell wasn't going to back Tom Johnson into a corner.

"She says he hit her..."

"What!" Tom screamed. "Are you fucking kidding me? His
right leg is broken, and his tires are under her front wheels. But the
lying little cunt is saying *TJ* hit *her!* Worse than that, you crooked
bastards are listening to her."

"Sir, I'm going to have to ask you to calm down and watch
your language."

"Bug and I saw the whole thing," Derek said excitedly. "She
was on the phone, and she pulled out and just ran right into him."

"I'm sure you saw all of that from across the street," the officer scoffed.

Tom looked across the street to the Taco Bell. He didn't see
any reason why they couldn't have seen it. The whole area was lit up
as bright as day. Hell, the stop sign was under a damn street light!

"You boys go on and get out of here now," The cop told
them.

"Did you take their statement?" Tom asked.

The cop gave Tom a look which said he thought Tom was a
fucking idiot, and Tom fought every instinct he had to keep from punch-

ing the asshole right in the face. He couldn't worry about this shit now. He had a hurt kid, he had to get to the hospital. He told the fat bastard as much and left.

Derek and Bug man left, too. They went up to Pizza Parlor to tell their friends Mike and Marty what happened.

"Tell me yer fucking kidding me, man," Mike said. "If this is your idea of a joke, it isn't fucking funny."

"Man. I'm not kidding," Bug Man said crossing his chest with his finger.

"Is he gonna be OK?" Marty asked.

"I don't know, man. She hit him hard; it sounded like two cars hit. Knocked TJ all the way into the suicide lane. His leg looks really bad. He wasn't knocked out, though," Bug Man answered. He was still shaking, scared by what he had seen and sick because it was a friend of his.

"Man, he's just a kid," Mike said. They were all just kids, but TJ was Kim's younger brother, so even though he was only two years younger than they were, that made him a kid.

"Did anyone tell Kim?" Marty asked.

"Her mom called her at work; she's on her way to the hospital I suppose," Bug Man answered.

"Who hit him?" Mike asked.

"Amy Ashe," Bug man answered there was a moment of silence then.

"That fucking cunt!" they all said in unison.

Amy Ashe's grandfather had been a crocked county judge. Of course, where they lived the whole damn judicial system was as corrupt as TV evangelism. Kenneth Ashe had been worse than most, or better depending on how you looked at it. He still owned a lot of people. The joke in town was that he was more powerful retired than the new judge was sitting on the bench. It wasn't a very funny joke, because it was true.

Amy's father had made a small fortune in business. Of course, no one really knew what that business was. The man had money crawling out his butt, and no one seemed to know exactly what the fucker did for a living. Maybe he printed the shit.

Amy got everything handed to her on the proverbial silver

platter. She did whatever she liked, and hardly anyone even *tried* to stop her. Those few who did were always sorry.

She treated everyone like shit except her butt-licking preppie friends, and they only stayed her friends as long as they did exactly what she told them to do. Only if they wore the right clothes, the right hair cut, and associated with the right people could they stay associated with *her*.

In short, she was the biggest bitch that any of them knew.

"She's trying to say *TJ* hit *her*," Bug man said.

"Your fucking kidding me!" Mike said. "Oh, that does it. Let's go get our girls to whip her ass."

"Our girls! Man, what the hell are you talking about?" Marty said. "We ain't got no *girls;* we're poor southern white boys."

Mike shrugged. "Mandy and Lindsy," he defended.

"Man, if they kicked that bitches ass they'd go to jail just as fast as we would," Derek said. "No one can touch that bitch."

Bug Man was the most contemplative and serious of the four. He squinted his eyes and leaned his head closer to the table top. They all moved in to hear what he had to say. "I might know someone who can."

"...Yeah, it was kind of spooky at first, Suzy," Amy said talking on the phone as she lay on her stomach on her bed. "But then it was kind of exciting... Like cops and ambulances and stuff, and it wasn't like I was *hurt*, or like I hit anybody like a *friend* or something... Oh, that kid... You know, Kim Johnson's little brother... Yeah, he's going to be fine; all it did was break his leg... I don't know. He's probably going home tomorrow; it's just a broken leg... Now why would I want to do that?... My Granddad says there's no way this wreck is going to get put on my driving record. He's not going to let those crackers try to sue us for every penny we have. He says he'll make sure the boy gets blamed... He should have been watching more closely, Suzy... Which reminds me. I need a teensy-weensy little favor from you... All I need is for you to say that you saw the wreak, and that he hit me... Thanks, Suzy, you're a doll... Who's going to believe those two losers over *you*?"

#

Bug Man and Mike stepped quietly into TJ's room. He didn't look good. His color was bad, his face was swollen, and he didn't even wake up.

"Is he all right?" Mike asked.

"Yes. He's just sleeping off the anesthetic," his dad said. "He was in surgery for three hours. They had to put two rods in his leg. They say his leg should go ahead and grow, but he won't be playing football. Probably not ever."

That was horrible because TJ was a good player. Best one on their team. The couch said he'd probably get a football scholarship for college. While Tom and Charlotte weren't poor by any long stretch of the imagination, a college scholarship would have been helpful if for no other reason than it would have given TJ a reason to want to go to college. It had been TJ's dream to play pro ball, and while he probably never would have made it anyway, it was a shame to have a person's dreams ripped away from them when they were so young.

"That bitch Amy Ashe is running around telling everyone that TJ hit her," Kim said from where she sat at her brother's bedside. "She's found like fifty witnesses, too. Some of which weren't even in the county when the wreck happened."

"Well, I know what I saw," Bug Man said.

"We've already hired a lawyer," Charlotte assured him. "We're going to sue them all -- the Ashe's, the cops, city hall. Every damn one of them. This is a bunch of shit. We have insurance, but what if we didn't? They'd be doing the same damn thing, and then how would we even pay the hospital bill? Those God damn people's little reign of terror is about to come to an end. It's about time the corruption in this county was brought to light. She's not going to get away with this. She's going to pay for what she did to TJ."

But even Charlotte didn't sound convinced.

Bug Man and Mike were half way across the parking lot before either one of them spoke.

"It just sucks," Mike said. "TJ's parents have money, but they don't have the kind of money it would take to fight the Ashes."

"My parents don't have any insurance. If she would have hit me, we'd be broke. Charlotte's right; they'd do the same thing. They don't give a damn about anything," Bug Man said thoughtfully.

"The bitch is going to walk away clean. TJ's never going to play ball again, and nothing's going to happen to her. I say we stalk her; find her out alone. Then beat her head in with a baseball bat and throw her down an old unused well or something."

Bug Man looked at Mike a little startled. Ole Mike was really mad, and he just didn't *get* mad. He knew Mike could never do anything like what he had just said; he just wasn't a violent guy, but the passion behind his words was real enough. He was fighting mad.

"You got any money?" Bug Man asked.

"Why?" Mike asked suspiciously.

"Do you have any money?"

"Yes, why?"

"Come on then, there may be a way to make her pay. Or at least get TJ out of trouble."

Amy stood for the photographer.

"Beautiful Amy, beautiful! Now look pouty. You've had a bad day, and now you just want to go home. Perfect perfect, now hold that pose. That should have it."

"Really!" Amy shouted.

"That should complete your portfolio," the photographer smiled. "You belong on a runway, dear."

"I can't wait to see the pictures," Amy squealed.

Her newly acquired agent beamed at her. "He knows quality when he sees it." she said. "You've got quite a career ahead of you, Amy. You've got face."

Amy laughed and went to change. Her mother helped her.

"Maybe you should go see that boy, Amy," her mother said. "They say he's hurt pretty bad, and we could go while we're out."

"Mother," Amy sighed in disbelief. "Then people will think I feel *guilty*, and why should I? He ran right in front of me."

Mike followed Bug Man up the foot trail. "I don't know how I let you talk me into this. This has got to be the craziest thing we've ever done," Mike whispered.

"I'm telling you, this woman... Well, my Dad says she's got powers. He says she never ages -- looks the same as she did when he was a kid. He says she brought his dad's hunting dog back from the dead. She'll cast a hex on someone for just a few dollars as long as she thinks they deserve it," Bug Man said.

"A hundred ain't a few," Mike said. "A hundred is my whole week's wages at Pizza Parlor. How come we ain't usin' any of yer money?"

"Cause I ain't got any."

"Well, in case you didn't know, Bug Man, there ain't no such things as witches and hexes and stuff," Mike said.

"If you really thought that, why'd you agree to do it in the first place?" Bug Man asked.

Mike shrugged. "Cause I've been wrong before, and I sure would love to see that bitch pay for what she done to TJ. I don't know... It's like what the hell else could we do?" Mike said. "I want to do something, and I guess if we killed the bitch we'd go to jail, and that really wouldn't help TJ out anyway."

They both stopped and got real quite. There in a small clearing just ahead of them stood a small shack made of sawmill slabs. Herbs were planted in pots everywhere, and there must have been hundreds of cats milling around. Yet it was neat as a pin, and cleaner than clean. As they approached they realized there was no foul cat smell about the place. When they were almost to the door, it opened, and they both jumped.

Mike had expected to see a skinny old crone in black. This woman was an attractive looking well-built red head of maybe thirty, and she was wearing a brightly tie-dyed wrap-around sun dress. Her blue eyes sparkled as she smiled at them. Without them saying anything, or her asking them a single question, she held out her hand.

"All right; I'll do it," she said.

"Excuse me?" Bug Man stammered.

"I'll make the girl pay for what she's done. Someone has to do it. And I'll throw in something for the boy as a freebie. One hundred dollars, please."

"Ah, all right." Bug Man handed her the money. She handed them each a gingerbread man, and then went inside and closed the door.

Bug Man and Mike started back down the trail towards their

car.

"I feel like I ought to at least have some fucking magic beans,"
Mike grumbled. "Well, I'm telling you right now I'm eating this fucking
cookie, because this is the most expensive cookie I've ever had."
Mike took a bite out of his cookie and stopped. He chewed the
cookie slowly, making happy eating sounds, as if eating the cookie
was an almost orgasmic event.

Bug Man stopped and looked at him, then quickly took a bite
of his own cookie. It was just gingerbread. It wasn't even particularly *good* gingerbread.

"What's with you? It's just a cookie, man."

"No. It's a *hundred dollar* cookie. It's going to be the best
cookie I ever ate if it kills me."

Amy had pulled into Sonic in her already repaired car and
told Kevin what she hadn't been able to tell him last night, and now
she was leaving.

"You know what your problem is?"

Amy, startled by the sound of a strange voice coming from
her back seat, damn near ran into traffic. She looked into her rear-
view mirror and saw that an attractive garishly dressed woman in her
thirties was sitting in her back seat.

"Who the hell are you? And what the hell do you think you're
doing in my car?"

"Teaching you a lesson," the woman said. "Now drive."

The car took off, and Amy found that she had to either steer
or crash.

"Now, where was I? Oh, yes. You know what your problem
is, Amy?"

"That I have a crazy woman in my car!" Amy screeched.

"You only see people the way they are. Not the way they
want to be. What a person is at the moment is never a true measure
of their potential. Who do they want to be? Who might they have
been if people like you didn't stop them from having the things they
have worked for? If people like you didn't soak up all the good stuff
that others have earned, many more people could attain their dreams.
You take and take and take and give back nothing. Everyone makes

a mistake occasionally. You didn't mean to hit TJ, but you don't really care that you did. You and your worthless blood-sucking family have used your money and your power to make sure that TJ pays for your mistake twice while you pay for it not at all. There's really only one thing you can't buy with all your money and power. True friends. TJ has true friends, and they want to help him. To save him from you. Just this once, you're going to get the short end of the stick. This time *you* will have to live with the consequences of your actions. Only then will justice truly be served.

Amy turned around to tell the bitch to go to hell, but the seat was empty. Her phone was in her hand, but she didn't remember picking it up. When she looked back at the road, there he was. She slammed into the bike again, only this time the rider came over the hood through the windshield right at her. His helmet shattered the glass. She felt it as the blanket of safety glass hit her face with the force of TJ's body behind it. Then the recoil pulled him back and he bounced off the hood onto the pavement. She felt warm liquid running down her face as if from a thousand, thousand tears.

TJ landed on his feet. Remarkably, he was totally unhurt. He ran to check on the girl. He started pulling the glass sheet back out the windshield as some other guy who had stopped just short of hitting the wreck started trying to get the door open. TJ finally succeeded in getting the bulk of the windshield off the girl.

"You OK?" the man asked TJ. "I saw it all. She smacked right into you."

"I'm fine. A little shook is all." He looked at the fellow and recognized him as the new county judge.

Judge Hendricks pulled on the door hard, and it opened. "I've called 911; you're going to be just fine," he assured her, even though he couldn't see her face for the blood.

She looked up at him and started laughing hysterically.

AND THAT'S JUST THE WAY IT WAS.

I worked in a salvage yard pulling parts for awhile, and one day a mangled wreck came in covered in blood. When I asked, my boss told me the owner had died in the car. It was sort of creepy working there after that. It dawned on me that this probably wasn't the only wreck that had driven its owner to their death.

So... I got to thinking. If a house can be haunted by the ghost of a restless spirit, why couldn't a wrecked car? I told my idea to Bill, and together we wrote this story.

Bubba has an interesting couple of days at work.

JUNK
by Bill Allen & Selina Rosen

"All right, boys, somebody's got to stay and pull a part. I got a guy who needs the tail assembly off the Corvette. Who's it gonna be?" Old Moe asked. "Come on, don' everybody jump at once."

Bill Ray jumped first. "Sorry, boss, I got me a hot date, and I don't want her to start without me."

Moe laughed and spit a mouth full of Skoal towards the trash can. It didn't quite make it; it very rarely did. "Reckon that means you get the honor, Jake."

Jake Chester held up his hands to protest. "No way! It's getting dark out there. Besides, I had to stay last time and part out that old Ford."

Billy Ray laughed. "Ah, come on, Jake, don't be such a pussy. The bogey man ain't gonna get ya."

"Eat shit, Billy!" Jake said. "I always have to stay."

"That's 'cause ya never got no reason not to," Billy Ray said. "When's the last time you had a date, beaner?"

Moe broke in. "You could have had the damned part out in the time ya'll spent fussing. If this is too much a chore for you to handle, I could always do it myself, and then two worthless dead weight employees I know kin go right out an look fer them a new job."

Moe started limping toward the shop.

"I'll do it," Jake said resentfully.

Billy Ray laughed. "See ya later," he threw on his jean jacket. As he was walking out the door, he turned. "You watch out for that bogey man now, Jake."

"You bite my ass, dick head," Jake said and flipped Billy Ray the finger. This only made the bastard laugh harder, and Jake was glad to see the back side of him.

"Jake, don't let that asshole get to you. Hell, sometimes at night those cars give me the willies, too."

"Yeah, sure," Jake said and went to get some tools out of the shop.

Jake put a couple of screwdrivers, an auto marker and a flashlight into his pockets then walked outside. Satan, Moe's Doberman, was chained next to the back door. Satan jumped and danced because he knew it was almost time for him to go to work. Jake gave him a pat on the head. He knew that those teeth that playfully nipped on his hands would rip a stranger to shreds.

It was near dark and getting cold as Jake walked through the yard past the crane and into the rows of wrecks.

Moe's Salvageland was a huge graveyard of cars, and at night Jake felt the weight of all those hulks bearing down on him. Every one of those cars had once been new, and their owners had proudly showed them off. They had carried mothers in labor to hospitals, they had taken children to their first day of school. They had served their masters until they had nothing left, and some, like the car Jake stood before now, had taken their masters with them to the grave.

It was once a candy apple red 1967 Chevy Corvette; now it was junk. Classy junk maybe but junk all the same. The car looked like an accordion. The engine had been forced into the passenger compartment, and the steering wheel was covered with something brown that had long since dried. The windshield was a spider web of broken safety glass.

It gave Jake the creeps.

Jake approached the car nervously. He emptied his pockets, turned on the flashlight, got out a screwdriver and started to work on the tail lights. Jake almost had the lenses off when he heard it.

"Help!" It was a woman's voice -- as soft and velvety as a butterfly's wing tickling your ear.

He looked up, then looked around. Jake could see no one. He shrugged it off and went back to work. Over active imagination.

"Please help me," the voice whispered again. It was just almost out of ear shot. Just loud enough so you could hear it, but not quite believe you'd heard anything at all.

Jake put down his screwdriver and got up slowly. He walked around the car and looked in all directions. It might be that fucker Billy Ray. This would be just the sort of shit he would think was funny. Jake walked over with his flashlight and looked behind a few junkers and into the car crusher to see if someone was hiding in the darkness. But if they were, they were doing a damn good job of it.

"This is bullshit," he said and went back to the 'Vette. He was certain that someone was messing with him. Jake wasn't going to give that *someone* the pleasure of seeing him react again. He was going to get this done and get the hell out of here.

"Please," the voice said.

This time he ignored it. He just kept right on working.

"Please, can anyone hear me? Please answer."

Jake stopped what he was doing and sighed. "Okay, I'll play along, Billy Ray. What the fuck do you want?"

"Oh, thank God! I thought no one could hear me."

Jake's blood ran cool. That wasn't Billy Ray. It couldn't be.

"What's the matter? Are you stuck in here somewhere?" Jake stood and started looking into the smashed hulks nearby. "Hello, are you in there? Hello?"

There was only silence, and the cold whisper of night. Jake quickly finished the job and gathered the part and his tools together. He had lost the auto marker, but he wasn't going to hang around to hunt for it. Moe could take the $2.50 out of his pay if he wanted to. Jake didn't care. He needed to get out of the yard and get a drink.

He had several. Jake left the Red Rooster Tavern around closing time. He was half loaded and had no business driving, but his apartment was just around the corner.

Aside from his buzz, he didn't feel any more at ease about hearing the voice in the salvage yard. There were a thousand questions rushing through his mind.

There had been no sign of Billy Ray's truck when he went back to the office. Of course, Billy Ray could have parked it off the main drag somewhere, then walked back into the yard and hid.

But it really wasn't Billy Ray's style, too much like work. Besides, the voice had been that of a woman. If Billy Ray could talk like that, he was a worse freak than Jake had given him credit for.

Jake didn't feel any better, only drunk and more confused.

The road was covered in a light fog that had descended while he had tried to get more tangible spirits to replace the spook from the yard. It made the journey home that much harder.

When he pulled in to his complex, there was a light on in his apartment that he didn't remember leaving on. Normally that by it's self wouldn't have been enough to even bother him, but he was already squirreled out. He wasn't about to walk into that apartment empty handed.

When he got to his door it was standing ajar. His stomach tightened up, and his pulse quickened. Slowly he entered, the tire iron held high and ready to strike.

There was a woman sitting in the darkness on his couch. She was tall and slim, wearing a skintight black mini-dress, with her long, red hair tied back in a tight pony tail. Jake couldn't make out her features as her face was obscured in shadow. Her perfume, like jasmine, tempted his nose.

Jake lowered the tire iron. "Hello?"

"Hello," she answered easily.

"Can I help you with something? This is my apartment." He looked back at the number on the door just to be sure.

"I think you will help me." She smiled a smile so bright that it shown through the near darkness in the room.

A chill went up Jake's spine. The voice was familiar. The hair on the back of his neck stood up with realization. The voice from the yard! "You!" he stammered out, backing up a couple of steps.

"Yes," she said and rose from the couch. She glided up to him and reached out to touch his face.

Her hand was pleasantly cool. It caressed his cheek and moved down his neck. At her touch, all his questions seemed to lose their meaning and be forgotten. All that was left was the sensation of her touch. He fell into that sensation as if it were a warm pool in which he was drowning, and he just didn't care.

Jake awoke as the light from the rising sun poured through his open door and onto his face. He opened his eyes. He was lying on the floor in his living room. He was fully dressed. She was gone. There was nothing left but the faint lingering hint of her perfume on the air.

Jake got up, closed his door and went to the bathroom for an aspirin. His mouth tasted like something died in it. How drunk had he been last night? Did he just dream her up?

He looked up at the mirror to see if he looked any the worse for the wear. Scrawled across it was a message. *555-1234 Ask for Helen*

Jake sighed. *Thank God*, he thought. *At least I'm not imagining things.* Then he saw what it had been written with -- his missing auto marker.

The more he thought about it, the more questions arose. Where did she come from? Where did she go? How did she get in the apartment?

If this was some practical joke Billy Ray was playing on him, he could play as many as he liked.

Jake went ahead and took a couple of aspirins. The headache was still there, but for different reasons.

He started to call the number, but he wasn't sure what to say. Damn! He felt like a pimple-faced teenager. His curiosity finally got the best of him, and he picked up the phone. He punched in the number, it rang three times before a man answered.

"Hello, Winslow residence," said the man.

"Uh... yeah, can I speak to Helen?"

"Who?"

"Helen, you know, redhead, good looking?"

"Who is this?"

"My name is Jake Chester. Is Helen there?"

"Listen here, Jake, or whatever your name is. I don't know what you're playing at, but I'm a busy man. So, if you don't mind..."

"I'm not playing no game, mister. Helen is just a friend of mine."

"How do you know Helen?"

"Well... I know this is going to sound crazy, but I was stripping down this Corvette at Moe's Salvageland, and the next thing I know..."

Winslow laughed. It wasn't a friendly sound. "So, you found something that the police missed, eh? Well, name your price."

"I don't know what you're talking about. I just want to speak to Helen."

He heard a loud click which could only mean one thing. Winslow had hung up on him.

Jake sat there looking at the phone for a few minutes wondering what in the hell was going on. Then he looked at his watch.

"Damn!" he said. He was late for work.

Nothing unusual happened at work. Jake didn't hear any voices., but he couldn't stop thinking about Helen and the phone call. It was by far the strangest thing that had ever happened in Jake Chester's life.

He'd been home about half an hour and was grabbing a beer from the fridge when the phone rang.

"Hello," he said.

"Mr. Chester?" the voice asked. It was Winslow. "It took me a while to track you down. Sorry I was so rude this morning. Please meet me at the salvage yard tonight around midnight, and we will talk about Helen. Thank you."

Before Jake could answer, the phone went dead.

At 11:00 Jake was telling himself there was no way he was going to meet a stranger in a dark salvage yard in the dead of night. By 11:30 he had on his jacket and was out the door. Winslow knew about Helen, and Jake had to find out what was going on.

The black Lincoln Town Car was already parked in front of Moe's when Jake got there. He slipped his tire iron under his jacket — just in case — and got out.

Jake looked in the driver's side, but it was empty. Then he noticed that the gates were standing open.

Oh no! Satan probably has his belly full of Winslow's ass!

Jake ran into the yard. "Satan! ... Satan? Here, boy!" He didn't see the dog anywhere.

He walked in farther, past the office and towards the cars. He tripped over something big and soft. It was Satan. The dog lay still and limp. It was warm, but it wasn't breathing, and blood oozed from a small hole in it's skull.

"Damn," Jake said softly.

"Poor doggy," a voice said from behind him.

Jake looked up and saw a middle aged man with gray hair and a black trench coat. In his right hand he held a stainless steel automatic pistol.

"Winslow?"

"Yes, Sam Winslow at your service," he said casually waving the gun.

"You ought not to have shot Satan. Moe loved that dog. Course I guess it was you or him. He didn't like strangers." Jake wanted to rip the bastards head off for killing that dog, but as a general rule you just didn't piss off guys with guns when all you had was a tire iron.

"I don't think Moe will be any problem. Now let's see the Corvette, shall we?" Winslow said.

"Listen, mister, I don't know what's going on here. I just wanted to talk to Helen on the phone; I ain't done nothing. Is she your wife or daughter or something?"

"Come on, let's quit pretending. We both know that Helen has been dead for a year. You are wasting my time with this nonsense," Winslow said and pointed the gun at Jake.

A cold fist grabbed Jake by the guts. If Helen was dead, who or what had he slept with?

This guy had to be crazy, but since he had the gun, Jake wasn't going to argue with him. He led the man to the Corvette. He'd never had a man pointing a gun at him before. It looked like a cannon, and Jake didn't want to do anything that might make Winslow pull that trigger.

"Here it is," Jake said. "You killed her, didn't you?" It wasn't a really a question.

Winslow laughed. "Of course. What's the purpose of this charade? You know I cut the brake lines, or we wouldn't be here."

"Why?" Jake asked.

"Jake, you know how women are. They take and take, and when they don't get what they want, they try to destroy you. I kept Helen in the finest. Fancy apartments, nice clothes, classy car, but it wasn't enough. She wanted to be Mrs. Winslow, and if I refused, she said she would expose our arrangements. All in all, I would have gladly divorced my wife to marry Helen, but my wife has the money. I would have been out on the street, and to tell you the truth, I doubt that Helen would have stayed interested in a poor, middle aged man for long. So, I fixed her brakes for her, and she went over a cliff. Neat, clean and efficient. Except for this car," Winslow said and thumped what was left of the roof, "... and you."

Jake paled. It was finally all clear. Winslow was going to kill him. Somehow he had avoided thinking about it all this time. Somehow he had believed that if he did what this guy said, he would be okay. Now he knew better. He decided to go for it.

Jake reached into his jacket and brought out the tire iron in one smooth motion. He swung at Winslow and caught his gun arm. The pistol went flying in through the Corvette's shattered window.

Jake tried to get a good hit into the older man's flabby gut but missed. Winslow connected with a cruel right across Jake's jaw. Jake saw blue stars in the darkness and fell back, stunned.

Winslow grabbed Jake, forced him into a headlock and began choking him. Jake lost hold of the tire iron, and it fell to the ground.

Jake bent to try to throw Winslow over his shoulder. Winslow lost his grip and flew off him. Jake reeled around and tried to clear his vision.

Winslow ran toward the Corvette.

Jake rushed forward when he realized what Winslow was after.

Winslow smiled, wrenched the door open and reached in for the gun that lay on the seat.

Just as Winslow was turning back, gun in hand, the car door slammed shut on his arm with bone crushing force.

Winslow screamed. His arm was stuck, and blood seeped around the edges. The gun went off once, twice. Each time the barrel spit yellow flame, and the bullet tore through the bottom of the Corvette hitting the ground beneath harmlessly.

Suddenly the night was filled with another sound. The crane's engine had started. Jake looked toward the booth but saw only dark emptiness.

Winslow was also looking at the crane's operating booth, but from the terrified look on his face, it was clear that he was seeing more than Jake was.

The great crane hoisted the electromagnet on the end of the steel cable to the Corvette and latched hold of the wreck.

"Damn it! No! Let go!" Winslow screamed as he and the car began to rise into the air. He was suspended by his bleeding arm, stuck in the door by an unnatural force.

The crane maneuvered the car and Winslow to the right. Suddenly Jake knew where it was headed.

Winslow looked down toward the gaping chasm of the car crusher. "No!" he screamed.

The magnet released, dropping its load into the crusher. Jake heard a scream that was almost instantly drowned out by the hiss of hydraulic pistons as the walls of the crusher came together.

The machine went through its cycle and then reopened. Finally, the night was still and quiet.

Jake's morbid curiosity got the better of him, so he stepped forward to the rim of the crusher and peered over the edge. Inside there was a mass of greasy hair, pink flesh and white bone crushed together with black clothing. It set in an uneven cube upon a pool of blood and bile. There was no sign that the car had ever been there.

Jake heard the roar of an engine at the gate. He turned away from the crusher and ran towards the office. As he approached, he saw Helen standing on the roadway wearing a white jumpsuit with a V-neck. Her pale breasts shone translucent in the moonlight. She wore wraparound black shades and lipstick the color of fresh blood.

When she saw Jake she smiled and blew him a kiss. Then

she got into her candy apple red Corvette and peeled out. The car disappeared into the mists of the night. All Jake was left with was black smoke from the burning rubber and the hint of jasmine in the air and on his lips.

AND THAT'S JUST THE WAY IT WAS.

So, we all have friends who are really nice guys (even if a little dumb), and they always wind up with the only bitch you know that deserves to be married to a wife beater. She drains all the fun from him and spends him into the poor house. She seems to find some reason to bitch if the corners of his mouth should even start to curl up. In short, she is a psycho hose beast from hell.

Bubba finds the perfect girl; she just has one minor flaw.

UNCLE JACK AND THE PSYCHO HOSE BEAST FROM HELL
by Selina Rosen

Family reunions can be dull as hell. But Dad's family reunion turned out to be just plain hell.

My sister Emily was nine when Mom and Dad loaded us and our always flatulent Irish Setter, Billy, into the station wagon for the long haul from Fort Smith, Arkansas down to Wichita Falls, Texas. I was thirteen at the time and mostly concerned with pulling on my pecker. A trip across most of two of the dullest states in the Union, in August, in a car with no air-conditioning, to go see a bunch of family I didn't really know didn't appeal to me in the slightest. When you added to that the fact I had to sit in the back seat with my sister who couldn't sing at all and insisted on constantly singing country western music — which I hated —and a dog whose farts could peel wallpaper, I was living in teeny-bopper hell.

I had bitched about the trip the entire week before we left, all the time we were packing our bags and the whole time we were packing the car. But since the car was packed and we were all sitting in the drive way ready to go, I had resigned myself, had stopped verbalizing my disgust, and was just snarling. It was then that my father; who up to that point had only told me to shut up about a hundred times, turned around and rapped me a good one up-side my head.

"Ow, Dad!" I screamed rubbing my head. "What did *I* do?"

"Wipe that look off your face right now," he ordered.

I spent a few minutes trying to figure out how to hold my face so I wouldn't get hit again. My dad didn't get mad very much, but once you had pushed him too far he'd tear your ass right off your body if you weren't careful.

"Damn it, boy!" he cursed. "This is the first reunion my family has ever had, and you're not by God going to ruin it with your pouty, surly, teenager shit. Do you understand?"

"Yes, Daddy," I said quickly, wondering if I was expected to look sad or force a smile. I opted for something in the middle, which literally hurt my face.

"Good. You'll see, TK, you'll have a grand time, and if you aren't, you'd better by God act like you are," Daddy said turning around and starting the car.

We hadn't even made it out of the driveway when Emily started singing, Billy started farting, and I got a God damned boner for no apparent reason at all.

The car had started acting up, and the trip which should have taken about nine hours wound up taking us twelve. My dad, always an economic SOB, insisted we eat sandwiches and chips instead of spending the money on a restaurant. To save time we ate in the car instead of eating at one of the rest areas when we stopped to use the bathroom — which we never did enough to suit my sister who had to pee every thirty miles or so.

Mother poured koolaid into baby sippy cups for us. An invention of hers that, in her opinion, put her right up there beside Newton, and that my sister and I wished to God she'd never thought of. Drinking from them made us look like grade A, number one morons. We very carefully drank only when cars weren't passing us, which wasn't very often since we never hit more than fifty-five. It's a wonder we didn't die of dehydration on that damn trip.

Now I had truly loved Billy till this trip. He played catch with me and was my friend when nobody else was. But as I sat in the back of the car with the hair shedding, drooling, atomic farting bastard, I began to wish he were dead.

Sound a little harsh? You try gagging down a dry bologna sandwich in a hundred degree heat with a dog farting in your face, and see if you don't seriously consider tossing the fucking animal out the window at least once.

By the time we finally reached my grandmother's house it was ten, and we all felt like we'd been run through a food processor on puree cycle. My grandma and grandpa were still up "waiting for us" and ready to visit. I remember the whole house smelled good — like cookies and cakes where she'd been cooking for the reunion. The air-conditioning was pumping, and I was cool for the first time all day.

I didn't really know my dad's parents; we only saw them about once every two years. But Grandma wrote us all the time and sent us really great presents at Christmas and on our birthdays, so we loved her much more than my mom's mother who we saw all the time and who gave use each a dollar on Christmas and our birthdays.

My grandmother hugged me, and then said what Grandmothers always say to grand kids. "My God, look how you've grown, Thomas Kane! And oh so handsome!"

I remember being surprised that she had gotten so old. I guess that was the first time I really thought about people getting older. Until then I'd just thought it would be cool to be in my twenties so I could drive a car, get laid, drink and do other cool shit. I hadn't realized till then how un-cool it would be to be older than that. Like, say, in your forties.

I was so upset by this revelation that I excused myself to go to the bathroom where I jerked off for a good twenty minutes. When I think back to the looks on my parents' and grandparents' faces when I walked out, I realize that they knew exactly what I had been doing. But at the time I was sure that not even God knew that I beat my meat.

We spent the next two hours taking turns showering and just visiting with my grandparents. When my dad's brother Jack showed up it must have been about midnight. Now you have to understand. Of all my dad's family, Uncle Jack was the only one we really knew.

See, Uncle Jack was a big-time loser. As such, he was constantly
losing everything and moving in with us till my dad couldn't take it
anymore and kicked him out. Uncle Jack was always at least forty
pounds overweight, had hardly any hair, and his face was one huge
acne scar. As far back as I could remember, Jack had never had
money, hair, or a woman.

So you can imagine our surprise when Jack walked in with
her. She was average height, a little over-weight, wearing a skin-tight
red dress that was way too short for her, and more makeup than a
Vegas show girl. Her bleach blond hair hung down to the middle of
her back and looked as if she had quickly run a comb through it after
having sex. She looked cheap and easy, and my little pecker got so
hard so fast it damn near broke my zipper. She wasn't a drop-dead
beauty -- wasn't a beauty at all, really. She was just unbelievably
sexy.

If that wasn't enough to shock the Pope into fucking a goat,
there was Jack's own appearance. He was lean and mean looking,
wearing a fancy Italian suit and rattle snake skinned boots. He had a
full head of hair, and his face was baby's butt smooth. In fact, at first
I wasn't even sure it was him. Then he smiled, and where he'd had a
missing tooth for years there was gold. I immediately ran to my seemingly prosperous uncle and embraced him. Then I embraced my new
aunty — or whatever she was. I rested my head between her bosoms and soaked in the cheap perfume in waves.

Next thing I knew my dad was hauling me away from her and
ordering me to go to bed. It was late or some such crap. It hadn't
been too late for us to be up ten minutes before, but now it was too
late. I went upstairs with my little sister, me grumbling the whole way.

"If it wasn't for you I could stay up!" I yelled at her hatefully.

"Me! It wasn't me that tried to get a face full of boobs!"
Emily shouted back.

I blushed and discontinued the fight. Of course I had to share
a room with her, but at least Billy was sleeping outside. I wanted to
sneak away to go listen to what the adults were talking about, but my
little sister would squeal on me for sure. I could catch an occasional
word, and I heard them laughing, but I couldn't hear what they were
talking about.

Finally, I caught a break. Emily was out cold in only a few minutes, so I took a peek out the window, and in the driveway below sat a brand new Jaguar convertible. I didn't know what had happened, but either Jack's luck had changed, or he'd started shitting money.

I snuck out of the room to the top of the stairs. It was a good spot; I couldn't see the rest of them, but I could see Jack's girlfriend. I watched as her cleavage heaved up and down with her breath. She had some really great tits — isn't any doubt about that.

"So, what do you do, Suzy?" I heard my grandmother ask.

She smiled then. A smile that even at that distance didn't look right to me.

"I'm an exotic dancer," she answered without missing a beat.

I could hear my grandmother's gasp of disapproval, but she said nothing.

"That must be interesting," my father said in a voice hardly recognizable. There was a quality to his voice that I had never heard before, but that I recognized none the less as lust. "What does that pay?"

"A lot," she answered.

Her voice was like a song you could listen to over and over again... No, it was more than that — her voice was the sound of a promise of desire fulfilled.

I, of course, got a hard on. I tried to ignore it, desperately wanting to hear how my stupid Uncle Jack had fallen into all this fortune.

"I was down to my last twenty dollars," Jack started. Everyone else was funeral quiet. "So I walked into the casino and plopped everything I had down on the roulette wheel on 27 — my old high school basketball number. Suzy came by and said *Let me give you some luck.* Then she kissed me on the cheek. The wheel landed on 27, and I won. I was going to leave with the money, after all it was enough to get me home, but then Suzy convinced me to let it ride. To make a long story short, I didn't leave that casino till I was a very wealthy man, and Suzy had agreed to marry me."

"How romantic," my mother said.

"Did you invest any of the money, Jack?" my dad asked,

instead of just coming right out and telling Jack that he was a major fuck up and could probably lose any amount of money.

Jack laughed, obviously not upset in the least by his brother's skepticism. "As a matter of fact I did. Bought a bunch of stock with it. Damn shit doubled in value over night. I'm a fucking millionaire, man. Suzy has really changed my luck. In fact, Thomas, I'm going to pay you back every dime I owe you with interest right now."

I couldn't actually see the money, but I could hear it, and I heard my dad's breath as he gasped in surprise.

"There's... there's twenty thousand dollars here! These are thousand dollar bills! I can't carry around this kind of money. You don't owe me this much money, Jack," my dad said.

"Oh, yes I do," Jack said. "All the times you bailed my ass out. About time I put something back. Don't worry about losing it, there's plenty more where that came from."

I was just a dumb kid, and it still didn't sound right to me. No one got that lucky, it sounded like bull shit. As if sensing my presence, Suzy turned and looked at me. Her eyes locked with mine, and she fixed me with an icy blue stare. My blood ran cold, my penis went limp, and I practically ran back to my room. I jumped into the bed and pulled the covers up tight. There was something unnatural about that woman. Suddenly she didn't seem nearly as attractive to me.

You would have thought I would have trouble getting to sleep what with all the strange things going on, but I was a kid. The bed was comfortable, I was tired, and my head had no sooner hit the pillow than I was sound asleep.

I heard a loud noise and woke up with a start. There wasn't a clock in the room, so I have no idea what time it was, I only know that it was pitch dark, and I was in a strange room with no one to protect me except my nine year old sister. All was quiet, and I realized it was my dream which had woken me up. I had been dreaming about her, Uncle Jack's girlfriend, Suzy. It had started off as a cool dream, her naked, me rubbing my dick up and down between her boobs. Then it had changed. She'd changed, not a woman at all but a huge snake, an evil snake trying to bite me. In the background Jack was chained to a wall screaming and crying. It was his screams that woke me. But it had just been a dream, because now the house was completely silent, except... Billy was barking.

He was barking like he did when he thought something was wrong. Dogs do that, you know. They have different barks for different things. I knew I needed to check on it, but I was afraid to put my feet on the floor. Except for my poor little confused dick, I was still very much a kid, and part of me was sure that if I put my feet on the floor something would reach out and grab me. In fact, if I'm honest, even as a grown man there are times when I wake up in the middle of the night and can't get out of the bed for the same reason. At any rate, I didn't go check on my dog. When he started to bark louder I almost forced myself out of bed, but then he stopped abruptly, and a few minutes later I was back asleep.

I knew there was something wrong when I came to breakfast. Coming down the stairs I could hear them all talking a mile a minute. Mom said, "Who would do such a horrible thing?"

When Emily and I walked in a sudden hush fell on the room. Everyone was still in their bed clothes and looked very weary and sober.

Everyone that is except for Suzy. She was fully dressed in a tight blue mini dress and high heels, not a hair out of place, not so much as a bulge under her eyes. She looked at me, smiled as if she could see my every thought, and I knew in that instant that the woman was not human. No matter how fuckable Suzy might appear, she was evil to the very core of her being. I quickly looked away from her.

"What's wrong?" Emily asked.

If possible, the room became even more quiet with Emily's question.

I sat down because I felt like what ever they were going to say I needed to be sitting for. "What's wrong?" I asked.

My dad swallowed hard. It was then that I realized my dad had been crying. Now my dad was just not the sort of man who cried on a regular basis, so I knew it had to be pretty damn bad. I steeled myself and waited for him to speak.

"Son, Billy, died last night," he said.

Emily immediately started screaming and crying, and my mother consoled her. I was stunned for a minute, and then the first thought that came to my mind was that the trip home was going to be a whole lot more comfortable. This immediately made me feel like I must be the worst person in the world, and I think that more than the fact my dog was dead was why I started crying. I didn't want to be the kind of person who was more concerned about my own personal comfort than I was about the death of a loyal and loving companion.

When we had all stopped crying I asked my dad, "How'd he die?"

My question was met with absolute silence.

"How'd he die, damn it!" I screamed. "I heard him barking, and I didn't check on him, because I thought he'd be all right. It's my fault!"

"It's not your fault, TK," mother said patting my back.

"Sometimes things just happen," my grandmother said.

"I want to see my dog!" I jumped up and started out of the house. Uncle Jack tried to stop me at the door, but I easily ducked past him.

Adults really do try to shelter kids from the harsher things in life. Sometimes, just sometimes, kids ought to let themselves be sheltered. My sister and I both had nightmares for years over what we saw in the yard that morning.

It looked like the dog had exploded. Blood and bone and entrails covered the front porch and sidewalk. Except for the unmistakable red fur mixed into it, you wouldn't have really known what kind of animal it was. The front wall of my grandparents' house was covered with words written in some strange language in Billy's blood. Emily threw up. To this day I don't know if I puked because of Billy's mangled body or because Emily puked first. I have to admit that I can stomach a whole list of things before I can handle puke.

The cops pulled up then, and my mother and grandmother rushed us into the house while Dad and Uncle Jack talked to the police.

When we got inside Mother gave me a glass of water, and I rinsed my mouth out. When I turned away from the sink I saw Suzy. She was watching what was going on in the front yard with a smile on her face, and I knew.

"That bitch killed my dog!" I accused pointing at her, so that there could be no mistake who I was accusing.

Suzy spun on me, her features unchanged.

"TK, for God's own sake!" my mother scolded. "Why would you say such a thing?"

She looked at Suzy. "I'm very sorry. He's just upset about his dog."

"It's all right," Suzy said with that same unnatural smile. "I understand. I had a dog once myself."

"She probably ate it!" I screamed.

"That's enough, TK! Go upstairs and get dressed," Mom ordered.

"But Mom! Can't you see it? She's not like us, she's..."

"Go. Now," Mother growled in that special way she had that said that if I didn't do what she told me to, she was going to rip my lungs out by way of my throat.

Not that she had ever physically punished me that I could remember, just that I was sure that if she did, it was going to be bad. Years of pent up rage and all, don't you know.

I went up to the room, grumbling all the way. I had just finished pulling on my pants when Emily walked in, so of course I screamed at her.

"What if I was standing here naked!" I asked.

"Then I'd probably throw up again," she said.

"Ha. Ha." I snarled at her.

She went over to the window and looked out.

"Cops are still there," she said.

I walked over and stood at the window looking down. Even from the second story window the scene was gruesome. The cops mostly seemed to be walking around in circles and talking into their walkie-talkies. Even at the tender age of thirteen I knew that the only place cops ever solved crimes was on TV.

"What do you suppose they'll do?" Emily asked.

"Nothing," I said with a shrug. "Cops don't ever do nothing. Sit on street corners eating donuts and pulling decent tax paying folks over for going ten miles over the speed limit." It came out almost like the canned speech I'd heard my father say so many times.

Emily was quiet for awhile, and then she said in a quiet voice,

"I believe you, TK."

I had no idea what she was talking about.

"Believe what?" I asked.

"What you said about Aunt Suzy," she said in a whisper. "I believe you. There is something wrong with her. I think she killed Billy."

At that moment, things between me and Emily changed forever. Till then she had just been my creepy little sister. She got me in trouble all the time, and she was always underfoot. That day Emily and I connected in a different way, and she never did bug me as much as she had before.

"Something not right about her," I said.

"She just kept smiling," Emily said. "Like it didn't bother her at all."

"It wouldn't if she did it," I added thoughtfully.

"But why would she do it, TK? Billy never hurt anyone... except maybe with his windys," Emily said. She moved away from the window then.

"Look at Jack. Suddenly he's rich, has hair, good skin. I'm just not buying it. No one with a track record like Uncle Jack's changes his luck over night," I said.

"Maybe she's a witch or something. That sure did look like witch writing," Emily whispered.

Someone entered the room next to ours and slammed the door. We heard people talking. Emily looked at me, and then I looked at her. Together we tiptoed across the room and stuck our ears to the wall. I recognized my Uncle Jack's voice first.

"Damn it, Suzy! We had a deal!" Jack said in a harsh whisper. "Just once I didn't want to look like a fuck up in front of my family. You promised me..."

"Jack, darling," she drawled. "Don't fret so. You're getting all tense for nothing."

"Nothing!" Jack screamed then lowered his voice so much I could hardly hear him, wouldn't have been able to if the walls in my grandparents' house hadn't been so thin. "Damn it, Suzy! You killed my brothers dog."

"He kept barking at me, honey. You know how I hate it when

things bark at me."

"It probably saw you for what you really are," Jack hissed. "Sometimes I wish I'd never met you."

"Ah, baby, you don't mean that," she cooed. "You were nothing till you met me, and now look at you — you have it all."

"Well, not quite all," Jack said in a low and unhappy voice.

"Quit your bitching, Jack. What good is a soul? You can't eat it, can't drink it, sure can't drive it around with the top down," Suzy laughed.

Emily pulled away from the wall fast. "She's the devil!" Emily gasped in a whisper. Then, with true nine year old logic added, "I'm telling Mama."

I grabbed her arm.

"We can't just go walking down to the kitchen screaming that our Uncle is balling the devil. That the devil killed our dog. No one will believe us; they'll think that we're insane."

"You're probably right," Emily said with a sigh.

"Besides, she isn't the devil. Everyone knows the devil is a guy," I said with brilliant deductive reasoning.

"Then what is she?" Emily asked in a whisper.

"She's a psycho hose beast from hell, that's what she is," I answered. "I heard about them in Sunday school once. You know, back before they quit letting old man Jetters teach anymore. He told us about these things called suc-on-us-es... or something like that." (Later on in life I found out they were actually called succubi, or in the singular, succubus). "He said they were like female vampires. They'd get all sexy and fixed up, then they'd lure men in and steal away their souls. Suck them right out of their mouths."

"Poor Billy," Emily said.

"Poor Uncle Jack."

There were about a hundred and fifty people there from both sides of my father's family that I'd never seen before. The family had rented a pavilion in a park that I didn't know the name of then, and sure as hell don't remember now. Even though the reunion picnic had started after dark, it was still hotter than the hubs of hell, and because it was night we had to contend with every mosquito and gnat in a four

county area. On thing that is definately bigger in Texas it the mosqui-
toes!

I remember looking around at this group of people and pray-
ing that I had inherited all my genes from my mother. Never before
had their been gathered in one place so many balding, beer-bellied
losers and their fat, ugly, matronly-looking, polyester-dress-wearing
women.

The Hose Beast was in her element, working these sex-starved
men like a fine instrument. She paid no attention at all to the women
who snarled and glared at her. She was feeding, marking her prey for
later. I knew it, and from the look on Uncle Jack's face, so did he.

Here he was. He finally looked like a big winner, but the truth
was that he was an even bigger loser than before. This time he'd even
lost his soul. The hose beast had used him, and now she'd throw him
out, probably everything she had given him — the money, the looks,
the hair — they'd go with her, and he'd be no better off than he had
been before. Worse, because now he wouldn't even have a soul. I
felt sorry for him, and I told Emily so.

"She's not even keeping her promise to make him look good
for the reunion," Emily said sadly.

I was looking at her. She was the embodiment of all that was
sensual, and she was evil, black and horrid evil.

"I wish there was something we could do," I said.

My "Aunt" looked at me then and licked her lips. My dick
didn't understand that I hated her. It betrayed me by standing up to
salute her. I looked quickly around to see if anyone had noticed my
problem, and realized that several others were having the same problem I was.

"The fiend must be stopped," I breathed.

"But how?" Emily asked.

It was a good question. I had absolutely no idea how you
killed a succubus. I didn't even know how to run them off. But
crosses worked on vampires, so...

"Come on," I ordered.

Emily followed me.

I don't know why I thought Emily could protect me, or for
that matter why she followed me, but I did and she did. I walked over

to the ice chest and pulled out one of the half dozen half melted popcycles that were left inside. It was a twin pop, and I handed half to Emily and I took the other half.

"I don't feel like eating, TK," Emily said.

"Shut up and eat it. I'm going to make a cross and try to drive the hose beast away." Thinking back now, I don't understand why I didn't just push the popcycle off the stick. But I didn't, and we ate them so fast we both got headaches. When I could see again I found a bread bag tie and made the popcycle sticks into a cross. Then, hanging onto my little sister's arm I approached the hose beast with the cross held high in my free hand.

When I was a few feet from her I started to intone, "Go away! Go back! The power of Christ commands you!" I think I heard that off *The Exorcist* or some damn thing. I didn't know what else to say. I remember wishing that I had listened harder in Sunday school instead of spending all my time trying to look up Carol Yardley's dress.

"You've got to be kidding!" the hose beast laughed.

Then, suddenly to everyone's surprise, she screamed. Then she made this gurgling sound. I thought I was pretty damn good at this exorcism thing, and then she pitched forward, and there was a wooden stake sticking out of her back.

Jack was standing there, his new suit and his once again bald head splattered in blood. He was laughing, and he gave us the thumbs up.

"Thanks for the diversion, kids," he said.

I kept thinking that the body would turn into smoke or dust or something, but it didn't. The Hose Beast just lay there bleeding all over. Everyone was screaming in terror. My dad and a bunch of the other men wrestled poor Jack to the ground, even though he was making no attempt to get away.

It kind of put a real damper on the family reunion.

My mother grabbed us quickly and pulled us away from the scene she would later blame for such ill-thought-out-deeds as my pot smoking and my sister's teen pregnancy.

Emily and I tried to tell the police what Suzy was, but they wouldn't listen to us. After the authorities heard Uncle Jack's testimony, he was acquitted by reason of insanity and sent to a mental ward. He hasn't been let out yet, and it's doubtful that he ever will be since he spends his days begging invisible forces to give him his soul back and preaching to the crazies about the evils of easy pussy and easy money.

And me? Well, before I realized that there might be something wrong with getting a hard on every time the wind blew, it stopped, and I had my dick under control. Now getting a hard on is like everything else; it's work. But whenever I have any real trouble, I just remember the Psycho Hose Beast From Hell.

AND THAT'S JUST THE WAY IT WAS.

Both now available in full-color glossy cover:

ANOTHER SIDE OF EVIL

Written by Jax Laffer   Cover art by Brand Whitlock

The crime that has yet to be categorized has finally happened!

Someone evil walks the streets of South Lake Tahoe, California. The police can't catch him. Psychiatrists can't help him. Some say he's the beast. The monster.

Most say he's not human. The unspeakable crime he commits, over and over again, comes from something deep inside. Something that's been handed down from generation to generation. Even he doesn't know where "the deed" will take him next. He's a quiet, calm, good-looking man, dedicated to the family business.

$14.00

He is Satan's nightmare. He is Joe E. Green.

THE LICKING VALLEY COON HUNTERS' CLUB

(A Martin Zolotow Mystery)

by Brian Hopkins

Cover by Brand Whitlock

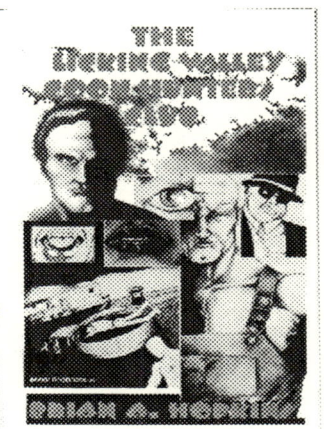

"...the newest edition to the adventures of Martin Zolotow delivers Brian Hopkins at his finest. Wise-cracking and eloquent, poetic and ready to kick ass at a moment's notice, Zolotow and his cross-wired brain are the perfect answer to a craving for suspense and mystery. Hopkins is one of the true new talents."
--David Niall Wilson

$9.50

Coming this fall with a full color glossy cover. Cover art and interior line art by **Matthew Scott.**

* * * * * * * * * * * * * * * *

Stories That Won't Make Your Parents Hurl

It's bed time. Like the excellent parent you are, you prepare to read a bed-time story to your children. What to read? Shall it be syrup or saccarine tonight? Or maybe we should skip right to the chunks...

There is hope! In the ancient tradition of the Brothers Grimm, Yard Dog Press is proud to be bringing to you *Stories That Won't Make Your Parents Hurl.* That's right! Coming late in 2000 is a collection of stories that will scare any 20th or 21st century child into behaving, just as those of the Grimm Brothers have scared so many previous generations straight.

No more sugar coating. No PC Garbage. Just plain, simple, *if you misbehave in this way, the consequences will be dire!!!*

Coming from YARD DOG PRESS in 2001!

BUBBAS OF THE APOCALYPSE

Contributors to be determined!
--Cover by Keith Berdak--

So, ya know what a "bubba" is? Know what the "apocalypse" is supposed to be? Now imagine that the end of the world comes in such a way that those off fishin' or huntin' -- or whatever -- aren't affected. Begin to get the idea?

Got your attention? Yep, we're reading for this shared universe anthology beginning in October of 2000. We plan to stop accepting submissions for this anthology on January 15th, 2001. Check the website for updated information. Guidelines available for a legal SASE -- one stamp.

THE HOST

by Selina Rosen
Cover by Brand Whitlock

In <u>The Host</u>, you will join Rabbi Tracy Cohen and her lover, investigative reporter Jane Weston, as they do battle with the undead in the streets of Jones Port, AR.

VAMPIRES ARE REAL, AND THEY ARE NOT NICE!

$7.00

FRIGHT EATER

by Selina Rosen
Cover by Brand Whitlock

The second book in *The Host* series, <u>Fright Eater</u>, takes place three years after the events in <u>The Host</u>. While Tracy battles Nazis & vampires and tries to find Jane so that they can patch up their relationship, the rabbi finds herself up against her most powerful foe to date.

Can she deal with her past, secure the present, and insure the future for the world?

GOOD ISNT STUPID!
$7.00

GANG APPROVAL

by Selina Rosen
Cover by Brand Whitlock

$7.00

In a big city ghetto, two groups of Soulless fight over turf, masquerading as rival street gangs and destroying the community arround them in the process.

Rabbi Traci Cohen and her rag-tag group of vampire hunters take on the inner city, apathy, and the undead in this, the most action-packed book of the series to date.

IF YOU EMBRACE THE DARKNESS, IT WILL CONSUME YOU.

Extensions

by Mark W. Tiedeman
Cover by Brand Whitlock

∞

$5.00

"Hold on. Just hold on."
"Nathan Frazier nearly died in the sleeper unit."

So begins the sage of the amazing life of Nathan Frazier. Follow Nathan through a labyrinth of emotional neglect, misunderstanding, half-truths and outright lies in search of the truth. You will believe the unbelievable and begin to expect the impossible as you travel in a straight line which is actually a circle.

Mark Tiedemann is a master story teller. Extensions is not just an entertaining sci-fi story, it is also an interesting perspective on human behavior.

Deja Doo $5.00

an anthology of the best from Yard Dog Comics
Cover by Aaron Henson

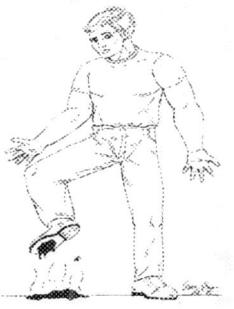

Visit a witch who helps you get a date by turning you into a slob. A couple struggling to survive in a wasteland of ice. People who talk to dogs, and cats that terrify people. Explore the origin of urban myths and the bizarre lives and burial customs of writers. Lose your keys and find an alien. Have a suprise reunion with a dead loved one and invade the mind of a crazed serial killer.

There is something for everyone in *Deja Doo!*

The Boat Man

Story and Cover art by Selina Rosen

"A Demon In Every Bottle."

Fact (News Week): In fifty year, the number of people over sixty-five will be greater than the number of people under twenty-five for the first time in the history of the world.

Detective Vickey Grip has never been very fond of the elderly. She blames them for every bad thing that has ever happened to her, and holds then responsible for ruining the United States. But even she would never have believed what's happening in the small resort town of Boiling Springs.

There's something in the water, and it isn't good.

$5.00

Shadow Heart

by Bill Allen

Cover Art by Brand Whitlock

Jake Blackthorne didn't used to believe in pure evil; now he knows better. He has only three days to keep the "Apostles" from trashing the world like they already trashed his life. To do this, he must find their hidden leader. -- Jimmy Ray Austin is sure he's doing the Lord's work, but who is he really working for?

DONT TURN AROUND -- THAT THING BEHIND YOU MIGHT BE REAL!!

$7.00

The Happiness Box

A Children's Book by Beverly Hale

Cover and interior artwork by David Kimmel

There once lived a very small princess with a very big problem that left her floating as a frail shadow unnoticed by anyone, even her own family. Find out how friendship and concern for others save the princess.

This story is masterfully told, an important book for both parents and children.

$6.50

(Quoted prices do not include S & H. For most orders, add $2.00
S&H per order up to 2 books & .50¢ per book after 2.)

Available at Amazon.com
-or- Order directly from us.
YARD DOG PRESS

c/o Selina Rosen
710 W. Redbud Lane
Alma, AR 72921-7247

-or-

srosen.lstran@juno.com
lynnstran@earthlink.net

MAKE CHECKS AND MONEY OR-
DERS PAYABLE TO *YARD DOG*
PRESS.

See our <u>free</u>
CATALOGUE OF GREAT
STUFF!!

Mail a self-addressed envelope with one first class
postage stamp to the address above.

Check our website for future projects:
http://www.yarddogpress.com

Printed in the United States
218686BV00002B/3/A